buddy's knife

edited by renate da rin

silent solos
improvisers speak

buddy's knife jazzedition, köln

imprint impressum

Publisher Herausgeberin
Managing editor Redaktion
Renate Da Rin

    Consulting editor Projektberatung
    Guy N. Fraser
    Editorial assistance Redaktionsassistenz
    Eva Nix
    Graphic design and Artwork
    Grafische Gestaltung und Illustration
    Jorgo Schäfer
    Print Druck
    Druckerei Hitzegrad, Wuppertal

© 2010 for this edition für diese Ausgabe
    buddy's knife jazzedition
    Teutoburger Straße 17
    50678 Köln
    Germany
    www.buddysknife.de

Submissions
We plan part 2 of *silent solos* and therefore encourage submissions from improvising musicians. Submission queries and general correspondence can be sent to the address above or emailed to info@buddysknife.de.

ISBN 978-3-00-030557-3

acknowledgments danksagung

The creative process of *silent solos* was guided by energy radiating from inspiring encounters, often beyond words.

Thanks to all musicians who contributed; thanks to Steve Dalachinsky and Herschel Silverman, who inspired me with their *Intervals*; and thanks to George Lewis for his insightful foreword. My very special thanks go to Guy N. Fraser for his very precious support and encouragement.

R.D.R.

> *Now is the time to know*
> *that all that you do is sacred.*
> Hafiz

Der Entstehungsprozess von *silent solos* wurde getragen von Energie, die immer wieder aus Begegnungen entstand, oft jenseits von Worten.

Dank an alle Musiker, die Beiträge geleistet haben, dank an Steve Dalachinsky und Herschel Silverman, die mich mit *Intervals* inspiriert haben, dank an George Lewis für sein prägnantes Vorwort und besonderen Dank an Guy N. Fraser für seine wertvolle Unterstützung und Ermutigung.

R.D.R.

> *Jetzt ist es an der Zeit zu wissen,*
> *dass alles, was du tust, heilig ist.*
> Hafiz

contents inhalt

contents inhalt

foreword

when improvisers speak, where do their words go?
George E. Lewis

In his extraordinary book*, In the Break: The Aesthetics of the Black Radical Tradition*, Fred Moten quotes the saxophonist Charles Lloyd, who responds to an invitation to comment verbally on his music by assuring his interlocutor that "Words don't go there." In response, theorist (and poet) Moten asks the simple and obvious, yet profound question: "Where do words go?"

I'm going to venture a different answer from Fred's, in admiration of his keen analytic meditation, and also in response to the collection of words in this volume. I want to suggest that wherever words go, they travel at the speed of thought, and they actually move faster than music. I can hear the musician's response: You hear sounds right away, don't you? Well, if you believe the neuroscientists, brains respond to sonic stimuli as slowly as a half-second after you hear them. That's not quite as immediate as some of us thought – but in any event, music, the interactive, dialogic structuring of sound by musicians and listeners, is another matter entirely. As the phenomenologists and music theorists tell us, music unfolds in both recollective and expectational time, and that process can take quite a while, extending deep into memory and involving lots of concatenative work.

Poetry is said to be the form of textual expression that most closely approaches the condition of music, but that identification is undercut by the infinite play of meaning that unfolds and expands word by word even before the poet has finished the first thought, but well before the musician has finished the first phrase. Even the most energetic musical performance, overfilled with quicksilver notes, rhythms, harmonies, and noise, is just poking along while its hearers construct its context, consider its meanings, and experience its effects. During that time, a single word, or even a word fragment that listeners can predict the direction of, has already generated a network of meaning in an instant. Thus, I've always found it ironic how the Watts Writers Workshop people were so influenced by the immediacy of music, when a simple haiku wins the meaning race every time.

But in fact, the uneasy, tricksterish intersection between two temporal universes that poetry-with-music inhabits is a source of hidden pleasure, a sensuous cleft stick that the improviser-as-poet must address: how to reconcile two experiences of time – none in remembrance, recollection, and fantasy, where indeterminacy and agency meet, and the other on a (now often virtual) page, operating in the interstices between immediacy and permanence.

Where do words go in an anthology of poetry-by-musicians? One imagines at first blush that a good deal of the interest in a book of this kind emerges as readers are implicitly invited to seek similarities and differences between a given text and its author's music. Certainly those additional pleasures are available. Taken as a whole, however, these texts also represent an international community of structures of feeling, where comfort with the style of storytelling that is canonical in African American culture is surely majoritarian, regardless of the so-called race of the writers. Some of the authors, like Jayne Cortez, are celebrated not only for their music, but also for the richness of their poetry, and its evocation of the relations among sounds, histories, and justice. Some of the improviser-writers in this volume make the valiant attempt to bring to the surface what many would feel more comfortable leaving as ineffable – using text to demystify inner states of musical feeling. Still others invite us to follow the word as it passes Milestones of history and memory – the beat and be-bop generations as symbolizing any moment in one's life that could never compare to any other.

Even though not all of these authors are acquainted with one another, they seem to share a love of jazz and the blues, embedded in a double consciousness that embraces the modernity of the urban landscape while distrusting its inevitable companion, technology, equally implicated in that double-star chiaroscuro. These texts are aspirational, pedagogical, spiritual; urgent, languid, nostalgic, and sensuous. We encounter lyricism, humor, signifying, and spontaneity; homage and remembrance of past heroes; homespun homilies, pithy manifestos, and cryptic words to the wise.

Even at a moment when the subalternity of improvised music is assumed in many spheres, this is by no means a collection of *cris de coeur*, but a convocation across generations, space, and time, in celebration of (as Yusef Lateef might put it) the pleasures of voice. All those words seem to be going toward an ardent, loving embrace of mobility and multi-voiced expression. As Lester Bowie declared in a 1998 discussion with another improviser-poet, Chicago Beau:

> "We're free to express ourselves in any so-called idiom, to draw from any source, to deny any limitation. We weren't restricted to bebop, free jazz, Dixieland, theater or poetry. We could put it all together. We could sequence it any way we felt like it. It was entirely up to us."

George E. Lewis, composer, improviser, and author, serves as the "Edwin H. Case Professor of American Music" at Columbia University, NY.

wenn improvisatoren sprechen, wohin gehen ihre worte?
George E. Lewis

In seinem außergewöhnlichen Buch *In the Break: The Aesthetics of the Black Radical Tradition* zitiert Fred Moten den Saxophonisten Charles Lloyd. Der nimmt die Einladung, sich zu seiner Musik zu äußern, wahr, indem er seinem Gesprächspartner versichert: „Worte gehen da nicht hin." Im Gegenzug stellt der Theoretiker (und Dichter) Moten die einfache, offensichtliche und doch profunde Frage: „Wo gehen Worte hin?"

Ich wage eine andere Antwort als Fred, aus Bewunderung für seine feinsinnige und analytische Meditation, aber auch als Erwiderung auf die Ansammlung der in diesem Band gesammelten Texte. Ich möchte die These aufstellen, dass Worte, wo auch immer sie „hingehen", in der Geschwindigkeit von Gedanken reisen, in einem Tempo tatsächlich schneller als Musik. Da höre ich schon den Einwand des Musikers: Klänge hört man doch sofort, oder nicht? Nun, wenn man Neurowissenschaftlern glaubt, reagiert das Gehirn auf akustische Reize relativ langsam, es dauert bis zu einer halben Sekunde nach der Wahrnehmung. Das ist nicht ganz so unmittelbar, wie einige von uns gedacht hätten – aber auf jeden Fall ist Musik, die interaktive, dialogische Strukturierung von Klängen durch Musiker und Zuhörer, ein ganz anderes Thema. Wie Phänomenologen und Musiktheoretiker uns lehren, entfaltet sich die Musik sowohl aus der Erinnerung als auch aus der Erwartung. Und dieser Prozess kann dauern, denn er reicht bis tief ins Gedächtnis und beinhaltet eine Verkettung verschiedener Fähigkeiten.

Man sagt, dass Poesie die geschriebene Ausdrucksform ist, die der Beschaffenheit von Musik am nächsten kommt.

15

Aber diese Beschreibung wird untergraben durch das endlose Spiel der Bedeutungen, die sich Wort für Wort ausdehnen, noch bevor der Poet seinen ersten Gedanken zu Ende gedacht hat, aber noch weit bevor der Musiker seine erste Phrasierung beendet hat. Auch die energiegeladenste musikalische Darbietung, übervoll mit lebhaften Noten, Rhythmen, Harmonien und Geräuschen, bahnt sich langsam ihren Weg, während der Zuhörer sich den Kontext gestaltet, ihre Bedeutungen näher betrachtet und ihre Auswirkungen erlebt. Während dieser Zeit kann ein einziges Wort, ein Wortfetzen, dessen Richtung der Zuhörer vorhersehen kann, ein ganzes Netz an Interpretationen erzeugen. Daher empfinde ich es immer als ironisch, wie sich die Leute vom Watts Writers Workshop so von der Unmittelbarkeit der Musik beeinflussen lassen, wenn doch ein einfaches Haiku den Wettlauf der Bedeutung jedes Mal gewinnt.

Ohne Zweifel allerdings beherbergt der unbehagliche und trügerische Kreuzungspunkt zwischen zwei temporalen Universen, den „Poesie-mit-Musik" für sich in Anspruch nimmt, eine Quelle verborgener Freude, eine sinnliche Zwickmühle, mit der sich der Improvisator als Poet auseinandersetzen muss: Wie bringe ich zwei Zeiterlebnisse in Einklang – das eine in Gedächtnis, Erinnerung und Fantasie, da wo Unbestimmtheit und Wirkung sich treffen, und das andere auf einem (jetzt häufig virtuellen) sich im Raum zwischen Unmittelbarkeit und Beständigkeit bewegenden Blatt?

Wohin gehen die Worte in einer Anthologie, in der sich Musiker mit Poesie äußern? Zuallererst liegt der Gedanke nahe, dass ein Großteil des Interesses an einem Buch dieser Art aus der ausdrücklichen Einladung an die Leser entsteht, Ähnlichkeiten und Unterschiede zwischen Text und Musik des Autors zu erforschen. Gewiss kann man daran seine Freude haben. Als Ganzes betrachtet stellen diese Texte jedoch auch eine internationale Gemeinschaft von Gefühlsstrukturen dar, in der sich sicherlich eine Mehrheit mit dem in der afroamerikanischen Kultur verwurzelten Stil der Geschichtenerzählung wohlfühlt – unabhängig von der sogenannten Rasse der Autoren. Einige, wie Jayne Cortez, werden nicht nur für ihre Musik gefeiert, sondern auch für den Reichtum ihrer Poesie und die Beschwörung der Beziehung zwischen Klängen, geschichtlicher Vergangenheit und Gerechtigkeit. Einige der improvisierenden Autoren in diesem Band unternehmen den bravourösen Versuch, das zum Vorschein zu bringen, was viele lieber unausgesprochen lassen würden, Worte zu benutzen, um den inneren Gemütszustand der musikalischen Gefühlswelt zu entmystifizieren. Wiederum andere laden uns ein, dem Wort zu folgen, wie es an Meilensteinen der Geschichte und der Erinnerung vorbeizieht – die Beat- und Bebop-Generationen als Symbole für jeden beliebigen Moment eines Lebens, der niemals einem anderen gleicht.

Und obwohl nicht alle dieser Autoren sich untereinander kennen, teilen sie scheinbar die Liebe zum Jazz und zum Blues, eingebettet in einer Art doppeltem Bewusstsein, das die Modernität der urbanen Landschaft miteinbezieht, während es gleichzeitig dem unweigerlichen Begleiter, der Technologie, misstraut, gleichermaßen inbegriffen im doppelsternähnlichen Spiel von hell und dunkel. Diese Texte sind das Streben nach Höherem, sie sind pädagogisch, spirituell, dringlich, träge, nostalgisch und sinnlich. Wir begegnen Lyrik, Humor, Bedeutsamkeit und Spontaneität; Hommage und Gedenken an vergangene Helden; schlichten Predigten, markigen Manifesten und kryptischen Worten an die Weisen.

Auch in einem Moment, in dem der Stellenwert improvisierter Musik in mehreren Bereichen nicht gerade hoch angesiedelt ist, handelt es sich hier keineswegs um eine Sammlung von leidenschaftlichen Appellen, um einen *cris de coeur*, sondern um ein Aufeinandertreffen quer durch Generationen, Raum und Zeit, als Feierlichkeit zu Ehren (wie es Yusef Lateef vielleicht formulieren würde) der Freude an der Stimme. All diese Worte bewegen sich scheinbar in Richtung einer leidenschaftlichen und liebevollen Umarmung von Mobilität und mehrstimmigem Ausdruck. Und wie es Lester Bowie 1998 in einer Diskussion mit einem anderen improvisierenden Poeten, Chicago Beau, ausdrückte:

> „Wir haben die Freiheit, uns in jedem sogenannten Idiom zu äußern, uns aus jeder Quelle zu bedienen, jegliche Einschränkung abzulehnen. Wir waren nicht auf Bebop, Free Jazz, Dixieland, Theater oder Poesie beschränkt. Wir konnten sie alle miteinander mischen. Wir konnten die Abläufe je nach Laune bestimmen. Wir hatten vollkommen freie Hand."

George E. Lewis, Komponist, Improvisator und Autor, ist „Edwin H. Case Professor of American Music" an der Columbia University, NY.

Aus dem Englischen übersetzt von Edward C. Sherman

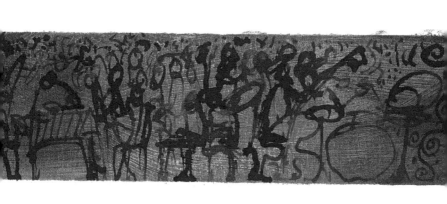

the woman in the black beret

In Lowell where Jack's heart still beats
    we gathered for some poems and eats
    the joy we shared was worth the cost
    Paradise was no longer Lost

    Paradisio's Found and so were we
    with music, song and poetry
    I'd done this six hour jam before
    the way Jack shared his open door

    Young and old came to hear and see
    the way it was and will always be
    when joy meets spontaneity
    all hearts connect and minds feel free

    On that October afternoon
    our trio played a brand new tune
    I saw someone come thru the door
    I knew I'd seen her face before

    She wore an old-school black beret
    but not in the Beat cliché way
    rather like the French still do
    like Dizzy did in '52

    Bird and Dizzy both told me
    that they knew someday they would be
    appreciated in the way
    that they finally are today

    It all took years and sometimes tears
    and they're not here to hear the cheers
    but their music's here to stay
    as classic as that black beret

Worn in a natural 50's style
that made all cats and kitties smile
when Bird and Diz and Monk were kings
with black berets and diamond rings

But Bird told me that Now's the time
to live without the Now's a crime
he said this back in '52
so someday I'd know what to do

Said "here's a thought for you to share
the hippest thing's to be a square
my beret's what I love to wear
cause I love Paris when I'm there

I don't wear it any more
other cats who do don't know the score
they think that fashion's what makes art
our music just comes from our heart"

Bird's words came back to me again
as I slipped from Now to way back then
but realized that Now's still the time
to share what's precious and sublime

and see that in some special way
the presence of that black beret
was Now the voice of yesterday
saying I'm still with you here today

Hours later just around seven
like a voice that came from heaven
the woman with the black beret
sang and blew our blues away

with perfect pitch and natural grace
she brought a smile to every face
we felt we were Now on a trip
as her voice sailed us on her ship

Now day was night I had to drive
three hundred miles to arrive
at my next port of call to play
some music on the very next day

I said goodbye to everyone
another festival was done
I packed my bags and paid the band
I hugged and shook my final hand

I went to say one last goodbye
to the woman who made our spirits high
I talked to her about her singing
and all the joy that she was bringing

how she made the precious past
alive and Now and built to last
and how her very special way
could help us all live for each day

inspiring us with her special gift
to heal all lonely souls and lift
our spirits and bring all joy back
as we all honored Kerouac

There was no more that I could say
we'd said it when we played that day
I watched her as she drove away
on dusky Lowell streets now grey

Laying there before my feet
on that rainy old-bricked Palmer street
resting there as if to say
take me, I'm your black beret

Now I'm on the road again
I really don't know where or when
I'll give her back that black beret
which she wore in that special way

She wrote me said just keep it warm
and wear it if you're in a storm
put it on a hook or on a shelf
till I wear it once again myself

I told my son when I got back
the way she sang for Kerouac
how when she drove away I found
her black beret there on the ground

Next year in Lowell where Jack's heart still beats
I'll bring my son for poems and eats
he'll meet and hear the final day
the woman in the black beret.

untitled

From the vastness of space
    To the empty-ness of zero
    I feel the earthiness of soul ... where anything is possible.
    SHINE ON, all the sounds and colours of the Universe ...
Play on, my Sisters and Brothers ... peace

28 January, 2009

forever

It is not just that sound is made of matter,
    It is that sound is what matters.
    Soundscapes are the key to our inner soul's door,
    When this door is opened we enter the Tone world.
    Life is but a fleeting moment,
But music is forever.

moment

The trumpet calls, I answer.
    Its voice is the one that I hear above the din of crowds.
    When its metal is pressed upon my lips,
    Flesh and brass become as one.

    The trumpet taps my soul,
    Releases my inner spirit,
    Strokes my sinews,
Bemuses my muse.

David Budbill

the subway philanthropist

The Emperor of Death loves only weapons and money
and so long as he is on the throne, The Subway Philanthropist plies his trade, prowling the bowels of New York
City moving deliberately from subway station to subway
station dropping fifty-dollar bills into white plastic five gallon
buckets, saxophone cases, violin cases, upturned straw hats,
Tupperware bowls, all sitting quietly in front of electric guitar
players, Mariachi bands, women classical saxophonists,
avant-garde jazz ensembles, brothers in do-rags drumming
on plastic buckets and tin cans, a woman playing a saw, an
electric organist playing Guy Lombardo's greatest hits, old
Chinese men playing one-string Chinese violins, Peruvian
panpipe players, young Chinese men playing Chinese flutes,
Buddhist monks playing Shakuhachi, doo-wop singers doing
close fourpart harmonies, conga players, bongo players,
cellists, string quartets, Hawaiian guitar players and trombone players too, all of them, every one, no matter how
good, how bad, it's music and it's a stay against, an antidote
to, The Emperor's hatred of all that is warm and good and
alive. And so The Subway Philanthropist plies his trade,
makes his rounds, prowls the subways paying one fifty-dollar
bill at a time to keep humanity alive while The Emperor of
Death wages war upstairs, above ground, in the sad daylight
of the world.

vision festival XIII
loisada, new york, june 2008

Home again in this silent place
  hidden on a quiet mountainside
  seven hours north of where I was.

  Home again to speechless tomatoes,
  mute green beans, dumb spinach,
  silent cabbages, voiceless potatoes.

  No more blare of car horns, sirens,
  jack-hammers, screech of brakes,
  busses pulling away from the curb.

  No more rumble of a subway train,
  rattle of a taxi, backhoes, pile-drivers,
  bulldozers, air conditioners, workers

  dropping plywood on the sidewalk,
  exhaust fans, workers dropping
  metal roofing on the sidewalk.

  Home now and away from all of that
  but home also and away from all
  the music too. Ah! Look, listen, see:

how music makes sense,
joy, art, ecstasy, out of
all that cacophony.

improvisation is
the jazz-mandala-voyage

For improvisers and those who love to sit in the center of the Cross Section of a jazz improvisation, it's the fearless ensemble-dive into the ocean of uncertainty that creates the "dramatic" tensions and releases – the compelling aliveness. It's the sense that a "question" could be asked, and there could be many different ways to "choose" the answer – and that choosing, in jazz, is often more like a surrender. So the music becomes an interplay of free will and destiny; a different kind of coherency.

You didn't see it coming. And there it is.
And you didn't see ... And there ... You see ... It ... There ...
It is ... Coming ...

Hearts ...

My choice of the musicians is based on their ability to man-the-vessel, to honor the "destiny" of a written song, its clearly marked form, the beams, the decks, the bow, the stern, the direction it's sailing or steaming in, and then enact their free will – from their hearts – upon it. These kinds of players service this certain musical aesthetic, which is to sink the vessel, let it go down, dissolve the lines on the canvas, and dive together. To swim, and to ride the backs of the whales – the plunging ride into total emorphous, loving, scary, and envigorating deep blue sea ...

It's like this – you stand on a sandy shore and witness the power of the breathing pulsing ocean. The vastness of musical possibility. The powerful waves undulate, rising, falling, slipping back under their own bodies. The horizon motionlessly crests against the sky far away. This is enough "story" for you. You aren't waiting for the plot twist.

You aren't anticipating. You are entranced. The seagulls are singing — you notice — they are weaving lace into the air. Any sudden swell from the surf, any distant thunder, any image your own mind offers, any sensual experience your body remembers or imagines only adds to the music of the witnessing at the ocean. It's all in. You are participating through receiving, and each exhale brings the next moment of the encounter as you give back by letting go.

That's the jazz voyage. The jazz-mandala-voyage. Anything could be "the event". No event is The Event. The Event is the event. The walls dissolve, the space appears. The space defines the walls. The walls define the space. The horizon defines the body of the ocean. The ocean defines the wave.
Music.

Put Tennessee Williams and Thelonious Monk together in a boat.

"The script is just a blueprint. It's the actors, directors, and designers that build the house," says Tennessee.

"Play the notes you don't hear," replies Thelonious.

The chart is just a blueprint of a territory and if it's a good chart, it guides you into uncharted waters. In the oceanic "maze" of the improvisation, the walls and space become not what you thought they were. When you improvise, you play the notes you didn't plan. The weather on the open sea changes. Winds blow you in new directions. You get lost, you find new horizons. The mistake, the dark moment, or, as Tibetan Buddhist Monk Pema Chodron says, the "seemingly negative-connection" is an opportunity for creative transformation, for "waking up" in improvisation. (Pema climbs in the boat.)

Jazz improvisation is like mixed metaphor. It's territory and boundary. It's politics. It's a card game. It's waves rising and falling. And in its infinite possibility, it invites you to find the spaces between the spaces; where space and sound is something you don't recognize, something new for you. Go where chance and intention are within the same hand ... a wave awakens you, offering clues to the beauty of life, love, and then ... watch your circumstances transform, hear what you thought you knew melt, see laws change and new ones emerge, listen as the boundaries shift, and receive your next hand ... what is it? It is ... What is ... There it is ... You didn't see it coming ...

swan song

Floating across the waves so deep,
    The moonlight shines in the night for all to see,
    Resting, I see that you will be my swan forever more.

    All of the time you have stayed close to me,
    Time it is now to float our wings up high.
    High is the night, we float across the universe,
    Feeling the flight, our swan is singing clear and bright!

    Floating across the universe,
    The swan sings out in the night for all to hear,
    Resting, I see that you will be our swan forever more.

    Time, it is now! The call is coming close to you,
    Now it is time to float your wings up high!
    Night, it is now, the light is shining, oh so bright!

Light, you are now so clear and bright!

sometimes

Sometimes I wonder.
Sometimes I think I know.
Sometimes I'm not so sure I know.
Sometimes I know I don't know.
Sometimes I really want to know.
Sometimes I just don't care.

Sometimes I think I ought to know.

Meister Eckhart said:
"This I know, that the only way to live is
like the rose, which lives without a why."

Sometimes I wish I kind of knew.
Sometimes I just don't care.
Sometimes I know I need not know.
But mostly, I wonder.

Mostly, I wonder.

kind of haiku

And the days would run from me
    When I asked them to
    wait a minute
    wait for me
Out of breath I walk slowly

the time before

Alone inside an empty room where shadows move across
the floor
And mingle with an ancient grace peculiar to a time
before
A distant laugh
A silent stare
The smell of perfume in the air
Upon the wall a regal gaze
Some royal heir of bluest blood
That melody begins to swell and float around my head
That melody I knew so well the time before
(the time before)
And suddenly I'm swept away across the floor
I'm in a trance
We're hand in hand and face to face
Our dance is one of ancient grace
Peculiar to a time before
Our shadows move across the floor

organic brown and sweet

We ain't about confectioner's sugar,
    But confections from the bee,
    Honey from the fields,
    Sweet, brown and sticky organic,
    Brown, sweet and drippy,
    With bits of larvae, pollen and wax,
    W W W W What's that, a bee foot?
    Foot of a bee in my
    Drippy organic brown and sweet?

And that royal jelly,
    That royal, royal jelly,
    Food for baby bees and food for the queens,
    For the babies and the queens.

That royal jelly,
    That royal, royal jelly,
    For the babies and the queens,
    Not confectioner's sugar,
    But confections from the bee,
    From the fields,
    Sweet, brown and sticky,
    Brown, sweet and drippy organic,
    With bits of larvae, pollen and wax.
    A bee foot,
    A foot of a bee in my
    Drippy organic brown and sweet?

Y E A H!

2005

old saint peter
(for peter kowald)

Old Saint Peter sittin on his throne,
    Saint Peter he be chewing on a chicken bone.
    Saint Peter looking down at you and me, smiling,
    He be smiling at what he sees.

Old Saint Peter how we miss him so.
    Saint Peter said, "Guess I got to go now."
    Saint Peter looking down at you and me, smiling,
    He be smiling at what he sees.

Old Saint Peter, he be travelling round.
    Old Saint Peter, he be homeward bound.
    Saint Peter looking down at you and me, smiling,
    He be smiling at what he sees.

Tell my friends I'll see them all some day.
    Tell all my friends I had to be on my way.
    Saint Peter looking down at you and me, smiling,
    He be smiling at what he sees.

    Saint Peter, he be strummin his bass,
    And making the case for being more human.
    Saint Peter looking down at you and me, smiling,
He be smiling at what he sees.

2005

keys to the city

Fascinating   compelling
          deep rooted
in the mainstay of avalanche boots
                    visceral mixes
the peacock spreading wings
          in memory of
poetry laughing to keep from crying
   & world bank trying to keep from laughing
all right   okay
                    get out of here
with your
cupcake brillo pad vampire-monkey-hairdo self
          great
          amazing
        compliments of the house
        one night stand
                jazz history
        sophisticated frogs
        hammerhead sharks
this is a great SM58 microphone day
in the taste of the smell of the fix of obscurity
          so many lyrics to
            write on broken guitars
so much electricity
to eat up
   and erupt into Lightnin' Hopkins
double time
half time
time of instinctive action
                out front
          in all stability
& multidimensional thinking
          a big asphalt storm
the road

41

restless
  obsessive
        ride you like a horse
into Tutuola's jungle
                turn you loose
& let you say why
        the French colonial empire fell
at Dien Bien Phu
        how apartheid came apart
at Cuito Cuanavale
        and furthermore
I have the trail
        I'm in the territory
I don't need the three stooges of jazz criticism
                to tell me anything
Frank Lowe has keys to the city of Memphis
play out
        play in
close the door
        open the line
harmolodicize & harmonize
        in the harmattan
                of your head

the mambo lesson

Yesterday took off its shoes
    and became an unpopular song
    today will end like a stunned fish in
    tomorrow's unequal distribution of
    emptiness
    as the sun makes its entrance
    without public support into
    the clairvoyance of your
    unsweetened panty hose
    & I am already
    smoking an image
    that will bite me
    before I change my tongue
    so don't forget your skull
    your fossil fuel
your utopian teeth

what's your take

If a two-headed goat pisses its
long piss of death for your
conversion into a free trade zone
If napalm is being buried in the ground
between tuner of concert pianos and
the pioneer of mathematical analysis
If the corporate terminology settles in
                    your mouth like a sweat shop
If a hyena shows you how to eat yourself up
& the blowflies blow your way
& you become like shredded flesh on
        teeth of the IMF
        Watch out
You are in the globalization economic domination process
        Now what's your take
If the world's most potent drink comes from
        juice of a festering sore called
institutionalized brutality
If the most extravagant treaty of abuse
sits like an occupying force on
broken body of an abandoned child
& if the political strategy is to be
        both covert & overt

at the same time at the same level
& if intimidation becomes a patriotic
        theme song called Intimidation
& responsibility remains a potty-training session
for all those holding their tee tees & wee wees
& if a newborn baby comes out looking like
        2 pounds of soggy grape
after a nuclear reactor meltdown
& if you find yourself radioactively depleted
invaded   bombed out   borderless
        dislocated   delinked
        Watch out
You're in the globalization economic domination process
        Now what's your take

finding the art of improvising music

Essential simplicity gives it to us.

The simplest expression of music is feeling. This feeling is dimensional. It has within it all my emotions. It contains everything I have ever lived. It is opened-out awareness. It is streaming energy. It is the source.

The simplest expression of musical creation is breath. Music is respiration, a constantly flowing exchange of energy with the environment that surrounds me. The music goes into me as a wave of breathing creative energy, rushing through me, pouring through my hands and through the keys of the piano, then through the moving parts of the piano action, the vibrations of the strings breathing, then bursting into the room, the sound on my ear matching the sound in my mind – all that in a split second.

The music feels like it pre-exists. When the energy flows through me, it takes on my configuration, my soul's imprint.

The simplest manifestation of music is the note. When my finger goes into the key, the key surface softens and opens. My finger gives way, too – no defining boundary of skin or muscle. Through the core of my finger flows the life energy of the note. Finger and key merge as one in the motion that gives birth to the note, an independent entity. This entity is very much alive and uniquely personal.

Lester Young called notes his people.

In one note is all the music I will ever imagine. Each note – a fully realized instant – is both infinity and eternity, manifested in simplest form. There are no boundaries here, only a continuity of pulsation.

When I create music in a performance, and the people who are there respond to the music on a feeling level, their feeling comes to me in an intense wave, goes through me, and affects the music that comes out of the piano. In this way, people who are there to listen actually become creators of the music with me. Their feeling merges with mine and the music is created and expressed by us together.
This feeling – the source, dimensional, with no boundaries on it – is love.

Marc Edwards

freer than free

I often check out musicians who play on the street,
There are many bands around so it's always somewhat of
a treat,
I heard a soulful alto saxophonist by the name of Wade
wailing on his horn,
I walked up to him and asked him to play with my band,
Wade asked: "Do you have music that you want me to read?"
I told him: "Yes, I like to use written lines."
He replied: "No thanks, I'm too free to be in your band.
I'm freer than free."
Freer than free, now that's a good one, I've never heard that
explanation!
On that note he turned and started screaming on his horn.

I saw this man about two years ago, and he was still
playing on the streets in the same place,
He started doing a very complex run on the horn followed by
a series of screams on his horn ending the madness of what
he played with a loud cow fart!
He smiled at me as if seeking my approval, but, I'd heard
what he played so many times, it wasn't anything new.
Not wanting to break the man's spirit, I told him,
"Yes, I know, you're freer than free!"
That comment made his day.

A fool living in a world that only he can understand,
As for me, I may as well be a stranger in Wade's strange
land,
Enough of these artists, most are crazy.
As I walked from the area, Wade was happily playing
unorthodox lines most folks would gladly call noise.

His eyes were closed as he blew into the alto,
he's returned to his imaginary world of convoluted runs on
the horns adding well placed cow farts to cap off an hour of
unfocused playing.
Poor Wade thought he was playing hot shit!
I guess he's hearing the inner music, the sounds that exist
only in our minds.

    Whatever happens in this life, I hope he'll be fine.
Life is too hard on artists in this era.
I walked away knowing that this man could do well,
if only he were more open to practical opportunities and not
condemn himself to hell.

21 May, 2008

Bruce Eisenbeil

blues in the road

You walked out of the oasis 'cause you wanted to steal my eyes.

You walked out of the oasis 'cause you wanted to steal my eyes.

You wanted to seal my mouth with dirt
but there was nothin' in the sky.

burning out sticky

Space and Distance anointed.
    The third party's impressive bite radius
    Implicates the rear final drive.
    Celerity conformed.
    Malarial eyes concordance.
    Toward the precipice – Black Cross.

    Burning out baby.
    Burning out mama.
    Total abjectness:
    Indifference – modern modern.
    Dom Dom.

    The voodoo and the hunger
    Bit down. She welcomed and
    Applauded the death of
    Just about anything.

    [(manipulate)]
    ma ni pooh la o la ani anipu pula ate

    The dreadlocks and the dreadnoughts.
    No forgiveness there man, not ever.

Burning out sticky on the banging porch.

Japan, December 2003

a girl on a purple bicycle

Exquisite for mind and spirit
Like being held in the arms of the clouds.

A girl on a purple bicycle ...

Valentine wedge
Flora charms bracelet in yellow gold
With malachite, sugilite and
Tigereye pendants.

A new Parliament is open for business.

Here on the Great Lakes, winter is served straight up.

A girl on a purple bicycle
Sees a blurred rooster run ...

All she had was Sunday money.
Julie was too busy to mind her own business.
Because the US is leaving Sudan in order to help it.
Are you a member of the Dollar Club?

In a neighborhood where
The streets are named after birds
A dollop of osetra caviar.
The dollarization of our Banana Republics.

Lessons in grit.
With an imprint of joy in his blue eyes.
It's a good life
To be an alpine skier.

Coming soon, nine million stories
In the crowded city.

Live who you are.
It's the only way to make sure that
Where you live says who you are.
They don't just fit you, these homes suit you:
A rare Victorian gem with your
Chanel suit and gloves.
Nothing says more about who you are,
Than where you live.

A girl on a purple bicycle
Sees a blurred rooster run
In front of a peeling blue house.

Venus is now shining gloriously in the predawn sky.

2006

Avram Fefer

an improvised life

The beauty that is music includes many different things
– tone, texture, story-telling, rhythm, love, culture, language,
melody, interplay, spirituality, and silence – all integral parts
of a powerful musical statement. Improvisation, much like the
practice of meditation, requires balancing seemingly oppos-
ing traits – focus and openness, determination and flexibil-
ity, consciousness and transcendence. The ability to flow
between these poles requires a combination of awareness,
intuition, and courage. In improvised music, there are times
when you must patiently wait and other times when you must
actively make something happen. And, of course, being able
to say something and having something to say is not always
the same thing.

There are two simple phrases being helpful in focusing
one's mind in this regard: one is "Be a product of time, not
the times"; and the other, "Inspire, and be inspired".

It's a subtle business, but even "free improvisation" has
some sort of structure. Being "a product of time, not the
times" means being able to say something that not only
reflects the momentary now, but the eternal now as well.
It requires balancing the transitory nature of means and
trends with the lasting power of message and truth. One
uses the power of the moment to tap into the wisdom of
the eternal. If you were a sailboat, it would mean using the
transitory winds and currents effectively to reach the under-
lying long-term destination, not to let them overwhelm you
and determine the destination themselves.

Older cultures seem to have the upper hand in this de-
partment, their music tapping the power of ancient belief
systems and the forces of nature. We Americans seem to
have the fearlessness and naïveté of youth, as well as a

belief in the supremacy of man, pushing them constantly towards the "new". The differences resulting from these influences are most clearly heard in the short immediacy of radio driven "pop" versus the long expository nature of the world's ancient "trance" music. Of course, ultimately, life and art require both of these tendencies to survive; this is where the delicate balancing act between *time* and *the times* plays out. Knowing when to *hold, fold, or be bold,* is the key.

The phrase "inspire, and be inspired" takes into account both the majesty and the brevity of our lives. It tells us to keep our eye on the ball and not to get dragged down into the trivial or mundane. It is great to find meaning and significance in the world, but it is equally important to let the chaos of modern life and the din of the crowd pass us by. Create community, surround yourself with inspiring people, and do the same for them. The trivial soon begins to fall away and all that's left is the substantial.

Another aspect of an improviser's life involves the potential isolation of one's increasing expertise. Here again, the trick is balancing the internal and the external — that is, who is your audience, and how do you connect with them?

As a specialist, you are faced with the paradox of the mountain climber: the further up you climb, the more you can see below where you have already passed, but also the peaks above and the difficult climb that awaits you. The tendency may be to constantly forge ahead without leaving a clear trail for the way back (where your less informed audience resides). That is fine if you are concerned solely with performing for other musicians or a select group of connoisseurs; but if you are interested in broadening your impact, then understanding your listeners may be of some importance.

There are two rewarding tools for addressing this particular issue: one is teaching, and the other is playing outside in the street (or anywhere else where you don't have a captive audience). Teaching allows you to relate to others, share your passion, and find a way to communicate your knowledge with people who don't have your level of experience. You are educating, building an audience, and expanding your perspective, all at the same time. Playing outdoors is another way to keep you honest and maintain your music's relevance. It helps insure that your music continues to touch and move people in ways that are not predicated solely on knowledge and experience of your particular genre, but also draws on a universal source. Both of these activities can help keep your music alive, rooted, and growing, while producing an art that is intellectually provocative, personally authentic, and emotionally powerful – all goals of any dedicated improviser.

untitled

... improvising is playing with your ears.
hearing inside and outside.
... playing.
                  letting the other one play.
... hearing what the other ones hear.
                                    and say.
          talking while hearing.
      being silent while hearing.
                  being at that exact moment.
present ...
    ... not before, not after.
                  playing while being.
                                    and being.
                  ...
          the happiness of now ...

standstill

Suppose people everywhere could become silent and motionless for a few minutes. All activity would cease. For a few minutes the only action would be observation. In these moments, one could hear the birds as well as the raindrops releasing symphonies of sounds. One could feel the breeze beautify, the sun, moon, cloudy or cloudless skies scintillate, and snowflakes sprinkle. Freshly viewed, inanimate and animate forms.

Heightened awareness of the senses.

Unconscious reaction could become conscious action. Greed, anger, pollution, prejudice, and war would be replaced by the obvious beauty of being. The awareness of just being could be shared by everyone. So simple, yet so complex.

The potential for us to wake up. Ah! Yes! The ultimate design. Notice, observe, love, peace.

untitled

A lifetime of dreams ... being fulfilled ...
    You have miraculously made them come to life ...
    your soul ... the dedication ... the passion ... the love ...
    giving of your time ... your kindness
    and honesty ... the swirling freshness
    and beauty of your presence ...
    You ... the listener ... the audience ...
    I am deeply humbled before you ... owing
    you so very very much of my life
    I love you more than I could ever express, in words
Thank you and peace be in your heart

child's play
a glance

Have you ever noticed how a kitten stalks a length of string pulled in front of it? Or how puppy dogs chase each other endlessly? Perhaps you have seen a nature film that showed bear cubs wrestling with each other.

Kittens, puppies and bear cubs playing is probably tremendous fun. Yet their child's play is honing their skills needed to live and to survive.

Their parents teach, train and guide them. God gives them traits that enable them to learn.

Have you ever passed your child's room and heard them talking with some imaginary guests? Maybe a tea party hosted by your little girl, the Socialite ... or a group of toy soldiers receiving battle instructions from your son, the General.

Communicating with imaginary friends is fun. As we all remember. However, it is also honing the skills for spiritual existence. You will have to teach, train and guide your child into a spiritual life, but God has already given them the traits to talk to Him.

Prayer is part of a spiritual life.

life speaks

Music,
> The language,
Love is my
> Redeemer.
Wisdom
> My teacher,
Nature
> My savior,
Living
> Is the stream.

Truth is only
> What is
>> And not
Because of one's
> Belief.

Seeing
> Is essential
In realizing
> Realities.

Pattern has to
> Be closely watched.
Intuition is a
> Vital aid.

Companionship,
> A flower of joy,
>> Is a seat
Of heavenly life.

True sharing
        Is instinctive
Of human beings.

Love frees all
        Who actually
                Embrace her.

Fear, a tool
        Of the devil,
Usurps
        Essential forces.

Integrity is the
Natural state of
        Being one's
                True self.

Fairness can only
Exist when all
Creatures have their
Own space by
Nature's law.

Spirituality is a
Way of communicating
With life's eternal
Love.

Family gives us
        The true meaning
                Of belonging
                And harmony.

Creativity is a
        Natural melody
And heart song
        Is the flowering
           Flowing
                Of love's voice!

The endless venture
        On life's moving paths
Flows in all directions
        At all times.
The giving of all
        Is one way to perceive it.
Then to see one's self
        Where one simply is at,
Not heeding such illusions,
        The want of this or that.
Then life speaks her truth.

2007

to see

Living this life brings
         Questions to be answered
Through the truth in our hearts
         Without demons of past generations.

Cruelty is to teach the child
         To fear what was – without
             The true wisdom of the past.
Faith cannot be enough reason
         To spoil the pure springs of young hearts.

Such offers only a life of hell
         Without experiencing heavenly truth.
Who could possibly be so arrogant
As to claim all are born in sin?
             Prove it, if it is so!
For there is no reason to prove
         False that which has never
             Been proven true.

Having been born in the jaws
         Of a vice does not mean
             One must accept its grip
             Of mental and spiritual blindness.

To see is the way of truth
         Not blind faith.

2007

you, my heart song

A whispering sound
       On a soothing breeze
Crossed a stormy ocean
       To tell me of you.

It seemed like a dream
       Though I was awake
As your chestnut-tinted smile
       Opened a heavenly gate.

To see
       Through the heart's viewing eye
            Without a wish of this or that
And feel the caressing of your thighs
       Thousands of miles from where I sat
Showed a mingling of our souls
       With endless loving stories to be told.

A heavy rain began to fall
       Playing upon my roof top
            Reflecting a sensuous call,
Pounding gently and strongly a song
       Endlessly singing on and on and on.

One huge, colourful cloud appeared
       Thundering, rumbling, shaking so loud,
            Love's pure passion began to speak
            Moans and groans
               Pure magical tones.

Intensities move towards heaven's gate,
Thundering hearts, a mingling slate,
Bolts of lightning striking each other
    Releasing the elixir
        Of life's nourishing ventures
           Into permanent paradise.

2007

improvisation – the celebration
of the moment

In German philosophy we know the expression: Music is
"entry to your soul". All that, what mankind calls since ages:
a r t, or the arts: music, painting, the spoken word, dance,
poetry, meditation, etc. are highways to your soul, formula to
connect with God, directly, without any sideways. No recrim-
ination, disaster and punishment. Because we all are a little
piece of God. Each of us creatures, matter, elements, minerals, plants, ...

We are the part of God, who tries to understand him/
herself.

The only way, trying to understand oneself, is, that you
want that.

That has to happen *before* you start on the long exped-
ition of self-discovery.

An artist works at it for his whole life, to understand each
moment of his existence and share this knowledge and experiences with the companions of his lifetime, communicate
in such a way, that they can be turned on to make their own
experiences.

The information in our art – music + dance – are readable.

The highest moments are those, in which a singular artist
– a musician, a poet, a thinker, a painter – or a soloperform-
er – or even better a whole group – much better: a *team*,
that are a few, playing well together people and musicians,
plus in our case, dancers, can improve their performance
into a group dynamic process of a mutual, spontaneous, only
in the spur of that particular moment of making, valid collective expression. Which, so to speak, bring results beyond
the horizon of the one, which a singular artist is not capable
to execute.

We earthcreatures improvise every moment of the day.
From our thinking to our actions, everything what we do,
is an everlasting process of improvisations.

Every talk we have, every thinking process, the survival-fight, our affections, love, each process needs our full attention and spontaneous actions.

Even a written down, fully notated orchestral work with exact instructions for the interpretation as we find it in the classical section is a written down improvisation of the composer. *Yes*, the *improvisation* is the most important and interesting part of our life. He, who is not quick-witted, looses in life and gets lost.

A musician learns in his life the many systems, styles and options of playing music together. As a "classical" musician you learn the high art of "interpretation", as a jazz musician you learn from the start, and that is the great attraction of this music, how you improvise inside of pre-designed compositions and styles (directions). If you look at this aspect technically, you have formulas and licks. Formulas and licks and phrases which result from the constructions and content of the compositions.

Same – like in classical music – if you have a special gifted musician, he learns his part by heart, a jazz musician does the same when he performs without a music sheet in front of him. He knows the lines, the phrases of the composition, knows the amount of bars of composition, 12, 24, 32, 64, 72, etc. in which the improvisations always repeat on the belonging chords, or their variations thereof, he invents counter lines, or substitutes chords and constructs, invents, varies with notes, which are in the scale of the chords or beyond, thus enlarging our hearinghabits playing notes and lines which are not in the guidelines of what notes to play with what chords, but which become meaningful by what the artist is "hearing" and therewith become extended chords and establish new hearinghabits, thus expending our knowledge.

It should be getting clear to the most unbeliever that a mutual expression is only possible, when during the creational process in a group of such calibres of musicianship and great people the chemistry among us must be in tune, it is ONLY possible when the ensembled earthlings add up to a powerful unity and unit which use their potential to work with each other with the fully awareness of each other's affection, trust, respect and love, and above all the fun wanting to make it happen.

It is not the form, it is always the content of the form which counts. And that is regarding the essential energies and forces here at work, a total worldview; an actual picture of the conception of the world, our planet and its position in this universe, who's context is gathered by the brain, the mind, the spirit (the holy spirit) and our senses plus all the unknown, all our feelings, all those things which change every part of the moment and take over new manifestations and influence our thoughts. The change is the only constant we know.

The fluctuation of the energy arising from the powers of our planet Earth and descending powers of energy we call the cosmic and universal energies, which keep everything in and around us in motion, and which flow through our inner body in a constant loving, creative birth-giving fertilization in a love-affair and loving-care of a couple engaged in eternal love.

Is our inside "sealed" by wrong behaviour (wrong nutrition, how to handle our body, unoriginality, imitativeness, trying to be someone else's personality), then we do not have any more access to our original creative energies and are sentenced to death.

Are we concentrating on our spiritual growth (nutrition, behaviour, love, empathy, consciousness and awareness), we are supporting and inspiring the creation. The goal is to be awake and aware at all times and being able to "give", to share. We have an endless flow of love, we can give, when we live in the moment (NOW), not in the historic past, but in the challenging improvisation of the "celebration of the moment".

untitled

stellar dust
we are
    in this form we forget who we are and our purpose and
our existence
you are not alone here on this planet
by the time i am writing this, there are supposed to be
9 billion other human beings on this planet.
9 milliarden (in german)
pretty crowded? wouldn't you think so?
tendency: growing.
this planet seems to be becoming popular in this part of the
galaxy.
this is, why there are changes. cultural changes.
naturally, there are forces who do not want these and any
changes.
there are always forces in charge.
nature of this planet has also its influences.
one of the things you should vision:
this planet is alive. like us. as a matter of fact, the planet
earth is our mother.
one part of our life energy is coming from mother.
the other is the cosmic or universe energy.
both make love consistently. i mean creation is coming from
the loveinterplay of the 2.
everything living on earth comes from these 2.

    someone found out, that we have 42 billion more years
of racing on this planet around the sun, before the sun feeds
on earth. that is the purpose of our home planet.

    the sun is a huge spider, collecting rubble and vitamins
and energy to hold with its incredible magnetic forces.

the stellar dust in its tow, like my spider in the kitchen,
who catches future food in the spider net.

so in 42 billion years we humans have to go and find
another disneyland.

but actually we are not here on this planet to see it as a
disneyland. we are caretakers. of earth. of us, of our species:
humans and all the other alien forms we house or are part
of, or will be still coming.
like you have a house down the road and many people come
by, passing or knocking at your door.

so now, each one of us. the humans. has his or her own
story.
each of us has different purposes, minds, spirits, or as we
say in jazz: body and soul.
that brings us to the music section of all of this mess here
on earth.
jazz music is the outmost creation. the expression of how
one feels.
i am just hearing billie holiday's voice. she suffers.
you think, only you suffer?
hear billie. willow weep for me.
the history of mankind, people treat each other as slave
master and slave, because they have different colour and
origin of country, on planet earth.

...

like the streaming water. like the endless energy of which
we all are part that keeps us on from when born to when we
die. the breath of creation. in our earthly case it is between
our home planet earth and the cosmic energy.

they have this affection with each other. the endless love
and its aim creation, birth. growing and gathering. experience. hungry for knowing, hungry for love, hungry for food,
hungry for sound. we feed on sound, as we feed on grains,
proteins, minerals, vitamins, calcium, salt, wisdom, no matter
how far we climbed the ladder of knowledge, there is no
end. as there is never an end to my music. from the first note
i heard, the first note i ever played until the last note, the
sound of my last breath will come out of this body, there is
a continuation of breathes, thoughts, feelings, musical notes
and clusters and human sounds and inhuman sounds, the
sound we do alone, the symphonies we do together.
we can create symphonies, songs, works, notes, feelings,

there are more different methods and conditions for
improvising than there are words to describe them.
the most apparent is to listen to each other and create out
of that moment collective music.
the more the listening, the closer the participants can get
into creating something fresh, something alive, something as
music, which is like the stream, ever-floating, nourished by
the breath of creation. not the imagination of it, but linked to
the original life force energy which is the creator, the foun-
tainhead of creation itself.
i invite you to be part of it and when you can keep up with
us, we will welcome you in our midst.
we give this knowledge to the children when we show them
the educational steps to play a music instrument. we start
with the percussion, the dance, the movements and the
connection to the body. the music we play, makes the body
move. the body movements make the music.
that's how my music always has been and will be. in unity
with body and soul. we understand while we are going along.
we learn from experience and listen and play with each other
...

within moments

I awoke to
movement
    a herd of leaves spiral upwards
    while a rushing stream collapses into silence

No beginning, no end
Yet ahead
My outstretched hand is
Transparent
A lens
that magnifies beyond reason

the road turns in upon itself
roiling a field of whispers
vibrations at each crossing
an unseen army
familiar and old as mountains

My gestures
Touch nothing
  only
      to trace shapes of recollections

        Everyone I have ever known

        And everything I have ever done

        And though shadows still descend

  Like oil sinking through water

        I am within moments.
        And I am not afraid.
        Let sleep approach.

2 October, 2008

a vision against violence
part I

... is a vision for the welfare of all beings
throughout the universe.
a vision against war, hatred, murder, rape, stick-ups,
robbery, wife beating, husband beating, children
beating, not helping the hungry and all the other events
outside of you,
your wonderful true beautiful being.
a vision against violence is a vision of seeing who you
really are, look inside and see yourself and find love for
your wonderful unique self. not the ego you, the true
you.
no violence against yourself means no jive ass talk to or
about others, no telling the unknown of the known to the
non knower. never boss around the planet means work
to save the wonderfulness of this wonder we call life,
we call spirit, we call earth home. a vision against
violence means to learn to truly love all beings, yes, all
beings.
no wars about religious faith, no wars about the food we
eat, no wars about the beautiful colour of the different
wonderful humans.
a vision of love – a vision of love – a vision of love –
a vision of love – for who you are will lead to a vision of
love meaning no violence. no violence. no violence.

here is an example of the vision of love for transition

for J.B. FIGI (Jamil)
the circle of light flows around us
as we all will surely meet again and again.

a vision against violence
part II

all those years shared here in this time remain
within the light of our love for each other.

we shall meet again and again in the sound of
joy, sorrow, passion, and wisdom of the music
of the word, of the movement of memory.

bright, bright, light shines as we reflect, recall
the quiet forceful power of the circle
surely we will meet again and again and again.

yes, we will come together to create the vision of love to
just sweep away the vision of violence that our world
holds so dear. love who – what you are from the
beginning until the end.

Om Mani Pad Mi Hum.
   NA MU AMIDA BU
   NA MU AMIDA BU
   NA MU AMIDA BU
   NA MU AMIDA BU
   NA MU AMIDA BU
   NA MU AMIDA BU
   NA MU AMIDA BU
   NA MU AMIDA BU
   NA MU AMIDA BU
   NA MU AMIDA BU
   NA MU AMIDA BU
   NA MU AMIDA BU

Terry Jenoure

blues in bolero

Music makes my mother do things
    And, in her kitchen Colon or Pacheco or Palmieri
    Or somebody like that
    Is blasting
    She stirs the pots
    She's dancing
    Can't stop if she tried
    Swooning how good it sounds
    Until I see clear through her
    Spirit moving in and out of every world
    Where there is no time

Music makes my mother do things
    Like forgive
    It's way down deep that she hears the Blues in Bolero
    It soothes and brings her to her knees
    This Bolero is her prayer
    The water and the blood
    That washes away bitter aftertaste
    Of day after day in this place that just won't grow things
    That without her song might even swallow her whole
    A Bolero that changes the direction of witchcraft
    Of the 'mal ojo'
    Curse from the merchants / the bitter old men and their
    pale sour wives
    Their spells broken now

Music makes my mother do things like forgive and forget
    I see how good it feels
    Her hips are stirring
    Back and forth and back
    Head tilt sideways
    Pots are bubbling and the water's pouring
    From a faucet that must have turned itself on

Music makes my mother do things like forgive and forget
    Here in her kitchen / her alter
    She dances
    Feet clap / feet clap clap
    She dances to break spells
    Feet clap flat / clap flat

    Then she covers every eye that ever cast itself
    down on her
    Gathers up every offense
    Breaks the chains that lock her to this tenement cell
    With a single sound, a chord that gurgles up from
    the deep
    Where she runs barefoot with the chickens and goats
    Dust on her ankles
    Mud in her toes
    The coconuts roll
    As the day turns pinkish orange
    In Mediania Alta in Loiza
    In her dreams
    In her pulse
    Her one song
    Offering to the Holy Ghost / Espiritu Santo
    Sacred name of all those women
    Before her / behind her / above her
    Those women around her / within her

These women with names:
Florentina / Jesusa / Cecelia / Candelaria / Hipolita /
Carmen / Auria

    Then the horns blare
    Tempo doubles up
    Inside her belly

That drum
As Bolero kicks way up high into Bomba
Pulse quickens and clacks
In the back of her throat
At the roof of her mouth
On her heels / through her toes
While she offers herself to Tumbero
Somewhere between *pa-gung* of the conga
And *ke-ke-ke tung* of the timbales
Flames rise
She throws back her head
Releasing her burden
Trumpets blast
Drummers break free
And Bomba swings like mad
She grabs my wrist
Sends me twirling
Her partner
My mother leads / I follow
And I learn to breathe
The turns and stops
Of the African throb in her joy
Like oxygen

no easy way

How fortunate those of us are who have chosen to spend our lives doing what we like to do!

Playing with others, when everyone is interested in listening to each other, as spontaneously as possible – and it is very possible, but not easy sometimes, if people are not interested in each other; as in all relationships.

There is no easy way to understand others' motives for playing; and, maybe more difficult to know one's own reason for standing in front of a paying audience and playing melodies that are not prepared for effects or impressions from the ladies or the many reasons that we try to justify our actions.

Opening my History of Western music I found a quotation from Aristotle (Plato's pupil) saying, in effect:
This is not a contest, just play nice melodies with nice rhythms, etc.

Also, he said, in effect, if you play and listen to bad music you will become a bad person, and good music will help you become a good person. Not bad!

More Muse,
Less Sic(k)

Peter Kowald (†2002)

untitled

Was da ist,
    das ist ja sehr viel,
    eigentlich fast alles.

    Ich höre
    sehe
    rieche
    spüre
    fühle: gut. Sammle
    pflücke
    lese auf – in aller Freundlichkeit
    vielleicht so wie die Sammlerinnen
    zur Zeit der Jäger,
    alles ist da,
    jedenfalls was da ist, ist da.

    Ein großer Sack (der kann auch eine Last sein),
    aus dem ich ziehe,
    alles auf den Tisch: was ich draußen lasse,
    ausschließe,
    wird zum Problem,
    lieber alles hereinholen (ausgelesen, ausgesondert wird
    später),
    wie Luft, Regen, Sonne, Kälte, Wärme,
    das was immer da ist,

vor mir ausgebreitet ist,
im Augenkontakt,
nicht übersehbar, im Ohrenkontakt,
nicht überhörbar. Nicht
alles im Blickwinkel der Ohren,
auch Niemandsland
der Wahrnehmung,
schwarze Flecken,
finstere Felder.

Aber trotzdem
ist da so viel,
so viel steht zur Verfügung
(dafür bin ich dankbar),
und ich versuche zu begreifen
und zu fassen,
zu nutzen und zu
lassen: nehme,
was da ist.

1994

untitled

What there is
    is quite a lot,
    actually almost everything.

    I hear
    see
    smell
    sense
    feel: fine. I collect
    pick
    assemble – benevolently,
    perhaps like the (women) gatherers
    during the times of the hunters,
    everything is there,
    at least everything that there is.

    A big sack (which can also be a burden),
    from which I pull things out,
    everything on the table: what I leave out,
    exclude,
    becomes a problem,
    I'd better include it all (I can sort out, select later),
    like air, rain, sun, the cold, warmth,
    that what is there all the time,
    what is spread out in front of me,

eye to eye,
cannot be not overlooked, ear to ear,
cannot be overheard. Not
everything is in the line of the ear,
there is a no man's land
of perception,
black holes,
dark fields.

But
there is so much there,
so much is at my disposal
(for which I am grateful),
and I try to comprehend,
to grasp,
to utilise and to
leave out, simply take,
what is there.

1994

Oliver Lake

befo' tomorrow

befo'
    tomorrow
        poems
    keep
dreams
    intact
           spiritual
necessity
    dreams
    returning
souls

if i knew this

hurricane force winds of desperation flung south

    southern eclipse of the gulf
    gulfed upward toward the people strewn rooftops in
    Nawlins
    Biloxi biloxi gone
    swam out of my attic to the safety of slow response
    government
    response laden with excuses
    continued ... continued incompetency and red
    red tape red blood
    blood spilled unnecessarily in the aftermath of a
    catastrophe

(please don't mention the catastrophe in Iraq)
where is the culture
where is the culture
where is the culture

    where is the culture
    bayou culture southern style culture
    where is the culture of life
    life is
    class valued
    poor / rich / poor / middle class
    on rooftops
    shouting rooftops exploding with fear & anger

    babies told to wait

    if I knew this ...
    stomach roilin ... with the sickness of helplessness

what can I do?
how far is my sphere of influence?

a 3 mile radius
from my home
to my family
to my saxophone

if I knew this ...

five part intuition

I am concerned with a notion of light captured by my repeated reflection that individual intuitions are not mere incidentals, but are active items of unity.

I feel and think that purity of thought is a natural human tendency.

And when at last you realize that the brooding stillness is no longer within your being, you will then experience the mastery of life's purpose.

Pure vision is the psychological clarity most closely related to that which is most Pure.

Light refers to the degree of understanding in a thought.

the bird

The bird flew down onto the ground.
    He chirped.

    He sang his song throughout the day.
    I marvelled.

    He sang of love and beauty.
    I listened.

    He flew away up into the sky.
        I remember.

le train
(vers Rome)

Nuit, rien, claque
    Du souffle, bruits
    Stop, du fer,
    Cri, claque,
    Deux rythmes, une toux
    File, rien, nuit
    Ballotté, le souffle, feu
    Nuit, crache, fort
    Rien, nuit, noir,
    Les gens, silence, du bruits
    File nuit, crache bruits
    Claque souffle, rien,
    Vite, nuit, rythme, noir
    Les sons différents, rien
Noir, noir, seule ...

Elliott Levin

song of solo man's psalms
(DIVINE-nation)

Fantasy ... Fantasy ... All is
                    (in) Vain ...
Take in names ... (of)
            GOD
            (damn!?)
                bless ... the
Same, by any other ... Nomenclature,
known as Nature ... or acts of
Greater or Lesser DIVINE-nation ...
Celebration of all facts and
theories of Creation ... stirs
a sensation ... regardless and/or in spit
of the evidently apparent
situation that we are what
we hear ... and here (what?!) we are!

Weary hard cold facts
in for a sweaty quartet
for the End of Time!
(... for the being) ...
                an eye for
an eye, that's all-seeing ...
To vie for the all encompassing
over(all)
view ...
        of where we may
    become aware, of where,
    at any given time, or reason ...
    a rhyme, to tease on
        the end and be
        of it all.

11 November, 2007

what jazz means to me

There is a distinction between art and craft. Craft implies mastering a specific technique to such a degree that one is competent enough to negotiate the general landscape of a given art form. For a jazz musician, this means sounding convincing using the rules, customs, signposts, etc. of the music. Art on the other hand transcends craft by communicating the artist's personal and subjective feelings in the chosen manner. Aristotle wrote: "The aim of art is to represent not the outward appearance of things, but their inward significance." Mastering craft is a necessary stage of the process ultimately leading to artistic expression representing an individual's unique voice and personality – the ultimate goal of any artist's quest.

Music is the medium through which I represent my deepest feelings and thoughts to the world at large. With music, the communication between the artist's inner self and the listener is immediate and inherently devoid of any hidden agenda because of the abstract nature of sound itself – unseen, not tactile, etc. Have you ever heard someone play resentful or selfish music, or even on the other hand caring music? The fact that music is literally in the "ears of the beholder" opens it up directly to the heart and soul of the listener. This is especially true in the case of spontaneous improvised music, the core of jazz, which is so direct in its communicative approach, honestly delivered without pretense. The true message of jazz goes beyond intellect directly to the heart and soul itself.

On a more abstract level, a spontaneous improvised art such as jazz magnifies the moment. The act of improvising implies that the past and the future are irrelevant. There is no time for value judgments or censorship when one is improvising. If only because of the amount of information which has to be filtered through during the improvisational process, the jazz artist must be in the now, one hundred percent present, or the communicative value, let alone musical discussion at hand will be lost. At that point, the jazz player must rely on past habits or future intentions rather than immediate feeling. In fact, a constant dilemma for a jazz artist is just that: how to stay in present time, psychologically and musically. This "being there-ness" aspect inherent in improvisation places the artist in a position to interact in several important ways – in relation to the energy felt from the immediate environment and audience as well as the very real musical interaction taking place among the musicians themselves.

From a totally different standpoint, jazz for me represents the ultimate synthesis of independence and dependence, of the individual within the group. Except for the occasional solo performer, the majority of improvised jazz takes place in groups of several individuals which at its core symbolizes participatory democracy at work in real time. Though jazz places importance on finding and expressing one's individuality, it also demands cooperation and teamwork for the greater musical good. There is a delicate balance between selflessness and ego, personified in trying to achieve a unified ensemble sound and equally, memorable individual solo statements that move the listener. Subtle social skills which are a prerequisite for any group interaction in everyday life are called upon in the typical jazz group, albeit using the language of music as the means.

Jazz performance requires fine tuning of the intellect intertwined with physical coordination on the highest level. The intellect has to have stored an incredible amount of technical and mathematical-like data in order to reproduce this information upon demand in the spontaneous jazz setting. Improvisation also demands immediate problem solving abilities to delineate the proper responses to both the musical challenges inherent in the music itself as well as the reactions necessary for handling the possibilities and consequences of group interaction. It goes without saying that manual dexterity, the range of which depends upon the specific instrument, is taken for granted. In common with some team sports, combining mind and body into a smooth and unified flow is an ongoing process and challenge for the improviser.

There is also the matter of simultaneously expressing thought and feeling. In a musical gesture, how much is a mental cognition versus raw feeling? Does the improvising artist know exactly what (s)he is doing every moment of the way? Does it really matter? In the final analysis of course it is the listener's reaction that is paramount but these questions do permeate an improviser's world.

The quest for an individual and recognizable sound or style emphasizes the concept of total freedom. What an audience is truly witnessing beyond hearing the music is the result of an individual's ultimate expression of free will. The rendering of man's primordial need and legitimate right for self-expression is potent and symbolic to all those who hear the music. The inherent "cry" of human passion in jazz as in all great art cannot be denied.

On another level as compared to other forms of music, classical, world, pop, jazz is an inclusive music borrowing from all sources, both the musical and real world to inspire ideas. Jazz musicians are by and large among the most welcoming of artists to gaining inspiration from other sources.

Jazz music conveys a positive energy that serves as a beacon of light for all to feel and recognize.

Originally written in 1980s; edited March/July 2009

Joe Maneri (†2009)

one

Flaull clon sleare
Rouve clanslika
Flautell lunege
Blausodoh fleeka Lasflowe
bloomplek

Peelah donrowflin
Laszdellohdoe
      Plan celati dohnblohn
Leelahlah sourn
    elf daupin

16 January, 1998

two

Mnume

                leee – blahmné

       lawss, lawn –

          Parfaunrr

     Tzi   bonedesklohff

Phlemrossehowll

     floskcahzbrew

dahahll delf

     Nawdt

blee – ell 'Larlyedoh

Floweryeh Derk blari

6 February, 1998

three

Pillvelednah
     Slomsleeuneloh
Rossnawlawk
     Tehpac zee
Yityee Vebernanh
  Bergall nib
     Emzellinsk
  Noldskira oktrab
     – roig – illianul
     lesarch /

Weshregni oregge
     viesseharlc
Tenlilg
     uke nod

untitled

Hope!
    What is hope?
    Can you tell the person whose
    rent or utility bill is due and they
    can't pay the rent with hope?
    How about the boy whose whole life
    is wanting to sell drugs like the big boys?
    How about the woman suggesting sex
    without standing on the corner?
    Or the people listening to destructive movies,
    Music, TV, books, etc.

    Hope is ...

    John Coltrane
    Charlie Parker
    Duke Ellington
    Roy Campbell
    William Parker
    Cecil Taylor
    Sun Ra
    Horace Tapscott
    Alice Coltrane
    Mary Lou Williams
    Coleman Hawkins
    Lester Young
    Art Blakey
    Krs-One
    Temptations
    Amiri Baraka

The Last Poets
Sonia Sanchez
Etheridge Knight
Miles Davis
Kidd Jordan
Fred Anderson
Lee Morgan
Woody Shaw
Lester Bowie

And many many many many more …

untitled

Let the music take u
    Let the music take u

    It can go many places
    Places that man 'n' woman
    Can never go.

    Music can do all that's possible
    But
    Most importantly
    It can do the IMPOSSIBLE

    Reach for not what u can do
    But
    What u cannot do

It's there 4 u.

untitled

What is real?   What is not?
What izz?
What izznt?
Our planet is so sad
That people will tell us anything
And we will believe
We believe hype of lost musicians
We believe hype of lyin' politicians
Of lyin' neighbors
So-called friends
Of political hopefuls
Who says what but
Not now
People who care u and use fright
To knock u out of sight
What is real?   What is not?
you know!

dream-time too quickly

we touched
    in dream-time
    you say, we touched too quickly

    finding each other in
    human scent, in
    heartbeat, in
    inner spaces, in
    the moment of discovery, uncovering
    layers cotton, uncovering
    layers silk, uncovering
    layers, head-trips

    we touched
    in brown toned nakedness
    the music called our name,
    we came together in
    one sound, you say,
    too quickly,

        we touched
        in dream-time

    the moment was
    molasses
    was
    sap dripping off a maple tree

    dream-time was
    my pleasure slowly ooooozing was
    our and interlocking in timeless stellar harmonies

we became sparking rhythms
flowing in
to the darkness of thoughtless formless bliss

dream-time was
years within seconds
dream-time is real

in separation we say, it was
too quickly
when the mind does its turning

the touch was
trance, was
not premeditated or planned

thought is
our anchor to the labor world
thought is
illusion
dream-time is
real

too quickly
is the afterthought
too quickly pricks my heart
quickly pricks needle pins that say – stop. loving. so. fast.

is love speed
is love tempo
is love
a driving undulating horn line over a running bass line
and shouting snare
bumping bass beat bottoming
the screeching rhythms of your mouth
in the to-be legend of rapture, your mouth
in its passion singing

singing for dear life
too quickly
your mouth on my mouth
too quickly
full and feeding desire
too quickly
finding flower petals in your feet
too quickly
arousing the spiraling life-force energies from our root

can we be blessed too quickly
vulnerable too quickly
the mind turns too quickly

if dream-time is real-time
and thought is illusion
real-time is magnetic underground and gravity slow
bottom heavy love
too quickly it is over

freeze time.

let us be real

reflection streams
(inspired by anthony braxton's
ghost trance music)

first it is dance with many hands,
    all voices one in the song of life,
    each a different temperature,
    a layer of the whole.

    it is a dance with movements real and imagined.

    intervals reflect the shining blocks of truth,
    branched into blood vessels of the mind.

    it is everything that any culture does ... participatory
    gestures ... children and a range of adult personalities
    engaged in building substantial needs from mother earth
    ... hands joining to celebrate workings in the big scheme
    of happening.

    clarity of society is revealed through
    individual decision-making,
    regard for others, and
    a common joy among its members.

    change. change. change is strange and surprisingly
    beautiful, then melts into the horrific:
    every changing changes.

    ultimately human,
    questions and answers sing in the soup of the mind,
    reverberating, bubbling,
    as sounds merge in overlapping dreams
    of the unbelievable and the familiar.

religion is bravery to BE.

moaning, laughing, dancing, interjecting.

it's a book to be read and repeated ... a culmination of
reward in the seeking.

all languages accepted and expressed with distinction
and space to hear them all.

it is pure honest genuine beauty,
ornate and shimmering,
a dew on leaves of morning life.

it's a book that opens a window in the mind
where fresh air can blow,
where anything is possible at any moment,
where instability is stability ...

it is a forest of timelessness
that is intelligence and love forever

Ras Moshe

albert ayler

Thank you for your songs of joy
    your screams of black essence
    your rejoicing spirits

    we still hear you even in those water rhythms
    we still listen to your spirit testimonials

    of what you've seen.
    Your message lives
    too bad you got so depressed at a young age
    you know Albert, sometimes you just have to say "fuck it"
    and just play your music
Jesus has enough money for now!

john coltrane poem #21
(dedicated to all the young people
i observe)

out of the south
    come human projectors of earth sound – on the way out
    there anyway
    the codes of grandma's lessons ("be careful when you go
    out there boy ...")
    we still try to watch it too
    beasts can still shoot you and then cry about apple pie
    and communism
    (Manhattan institutes of shame)
    but no matter
    John's music lives on
    a sound that speaks of
    the course of the stars
    as well as white hood cowardice.
    if each little black kid who got mentally slapped by the
    ignorant
    heard this music
    the life they live of confusion and violence would be only
    a past memory ...
    Peace On Earth Meditations Transition Kulu Se Mama
    (the drum ode)
    thank you John Coltrane
    for your energy
the soundtrack of life's constant moving in spite of ...

you are your own leader
(for walter rodney)

no pictures
    of the mystic king
    are on my walls/halls of memory
    no odes to the benefits of tithes
    no song chants for the prince of mystery
    I know about a music that speaks the truth
    and what we have to do NOW
    to move forward
in this movement

charles' song
(for charles gayle)

It's a matter of distance
    The mind takes its journey
    and calls that shorthand love –
    or a virtual representation
    of force – or maybe
    a relief map of pain
    Either way, Charles is our guide
    through these flat hot thickets
    Illegal as immigrant neurons
    we roll around our Texas Jumble –
    eyes peeled for John Law

    He keeps us fit
    by sending notes to
    scout the senses
    lifts 'em out of plastic saxophones
    and lays 'em down flat
    massages 'em with breath
    so they break apart just so
    tags 'em
    then sends 'em back to the wild
    where Scandinavian flight attendants
    hold their sweaty hands
    so they don't get lost

    But these proud buggers roll away
    unseen, a job yet unfinished
    Exhausted, they coax us
    down runways and
    onto the sacred corner
    of the today page –
    right there by the two-bar rest
    that wears its upturned fermata
just like a holiday hat

Bern Nix

man's condition

an attempt
    to transcend
    the
    banality
    and
    painful temporality inherent
    in humanity's
    seemingly irrevocable condition
    is implicit
    in every creative act.
    Artistic
    activity
    no matter how base
    or magnanimous,
    is
    a strategy
    employed to cheat
    drowsy
death

spring song for autumn

Spring
was homeless and her left pocket was greasy
like the brown bags used at Shirley's place
Oliver Malave sometimes known as the voice of reason is
changing the oil on Jessie Benjamin's red 1964 Chevy Impala
Jessie takes numbers and likes things to run smoothly
Windmill, also known as Lester Torres, stands at the end of
the street rotating his arms like the hands of a clock
A message is written across the forehead of the sun
A weakened ocean weeps while bleeding stars swing back
and forth between the Claremont and Paterson projects
the sky will still be beautiful
The sky over Rwanda, Bosnia, Sudan, will still be beautiful
even as gruesome murders are happening
As children rape their mothers while their fathers turn green
sons
Inside that sky beauty are voices that scream from the top of
their lungs
Every second of every day since the beginning of life
this beauty exists to inspire us it is saying
STOP!! ... do not kill that boy do not kill that woman or those
children STOP!

Capitalism, and patriotism have dumbed us down so we
cannot see or feel
We cannot hear Tommy Peoples
crying on those hot summer nights
while his mom is out getting her head tight
and his dad is nowhere in sight
Spring jumped up but there was a noose around her neck
the red, white and blue people had arrived
who he was that walked past her laughing
in a dim dawn ... soon gone
to find the entrance to the shadow world

un-aware it is a space only for the sighted
She was trying to find love
thinking Bob or Joe was the true one she let her guard down
on a dark Saturday afternoon
and Gary or Cary or Alfred
violating her soul
leaving her pregnant and cold
without a place to stay
now Tom or Tim or Sal didn't want to have anything to do
with that bay-bee
so Spring spat up an unknown future
when she forgave him that is Walter or Teddy or what ever
his name was
he didn't realize the gift he had been given because
throughout his life he fucked many women and didn't think
twice about it
he said I do what men do, I'm a man
the next morning I heard this shouting
one day I heard this shouting

We got spring! we got spring! we got her now!
there are over 270,000 species of flowers
they all sang at the same time
can you record that sound, that truth
can that become a hit?
in your world?
Sitting by the window looking
at those who step on flowers and wait for them die
who never notice the color
of their own children's eyes
creatures of the night
those who only see in black or white
who are always wrong but think they're right
those who hire others to start their fights
killing some people named
Malik which means angel, Huma which means bird
who sings and Jamal which means beauty

Although they neglected to tell these hired thugs that Malik,
Huma and Jamal are all under 10 years old
a few days before the sadness sea monster swallowed
everything in town, it was all part of the lost yesterday
WHO! HE WAS THAT WALKED PAST HER LAUGHING
that bright morning Monday
who he was thought he was better than the people who
dance on their hands
telling me who can and who can't make plans for tomorrow
and who is going to live another day

    That's all they wanted to know was
where is that piano player who wore the overcoat in the
middle of summer when the sky had a mouth full of sunset
and Harlem was still Harlem
they wanted to know if a cat could always land on its feet
and
how I is dead but still alive
and how I sold out to bounty hunters
Who looked for escaped rainbows?
You mean the stair steps, the heartbeats, the jitterbugs?
No I mean the ones called human being the ones who wrote
that book of cruelty who are now on the best seller list
It was Halloween and I disguised myself as a B flat Blues
I entered the club at 7am mister Big was cleaning the mess
from his noise when I looked out the window where
broken bottles and garbage lay
I see these geese flying over a lake
You know the one that fills with light every evening
when the moon comes up you can see just before the
sunrises
I knew I was here two or three befores
before I was born
before sound opened the doors of the Cathedral
and before I died
I'd like to hear, see and hold all the dreams that got away just
one more time

until the sky turns black
And maybe there is time to see the blue mountain
the one that hangs over the waterfall
If I could only see that one more time
If I could touch my mother's face
And if there are a few seconds on the clock
I'd like to go to the playground and listen to those feet
Remember that one little girl the one with bells on her ankles
I will know it is time to get to the essence
to finale
and let the memories turn to smoke
when I really listen I can hear the sound of trees coming
out of saxophones, trumpets and violins
it is same song the sky is singing
sometimes I can't tell the beginning from the middle or the end
is that what eternity is?

"Notes from a dedication to G.L."

    Thank you nice lady from Boston for
The grace
The strength
The beauty
Thank you for the invitation to complete the circle
Thank you for being host
To the Muse ... ic
for inviting the angels
the good angels
and
the naughty angels
the seekers, the visionaries, the poets
the ones with sacks of coal on their backs who scream and
shout
    but also those who go inside rainbows and cornfields
who play that magnificent music of hope?
from dust till dawn
The earth opens up to swallow itself and all that is left are

the memories of you and this unbelievable thing called life,
called love, called music that called you
to do this beautiful thing
Nice lady from Boston
the one who reminds me of that actress Audrey Hepburn
the one who looks like a sunflower?
in a field of daisies
    Then one day we hear that she is about to take this
music called life to another level
and we say
Not yet!
Not yet!
One more blossom is coming
One more winter
One more spring
One more summer
Keep fighting!
Keep Fighting!!
Keep dancing!!
Keep singing
Keep swinging
Keep fighting!
Keep Fighting!!
Keep talking
Keep walking
Keep fighting!
Keep Fighting!!
Keep dancing!!
Keep Dancing!

    (Birth)
Brightness again
she moves into brightness that we cannot stop
that we cannot interfere with
she is no longer
she is now the sound itself
eternal

Matana Roberts

it rained a fortune

Jetting down the runway
    of an icy jagged mountain in my mind
    never to release myself from its pernicious clutches
    always in a perpetual bind

    Hour by hour it took me
    riding on faint hints of stale air
    any could reach out and touch you
    in a grand colossus of thick black hair

    Not for one, two or three centuries
    feeling its hands on my throat
    over and over it taught me
    rivers and rivers of hope

    Take all that you must give me
    under the blankets of care
    never please never do doubt me
even if it seems unfair

in between gigs ...
... can you dig ...?

When the bandstand has been vacated,
   the musically medicated have left
   intoxicated,
   reconfigured ... renewed
   reborn ... again ...
   while lingering spirits
   of a charged magnetic field
   produced by the breath of wise men
   still hover before being absorbed
   into the cracks and corners in
   half empty daytime bars
   amidst afternoon drinkers and
   thinkers discussing sports, politics,
   and the day's breaking news.

   While the magnetic field of an
   unseen molecular alignment
   charged from the night before
   swirls in braided strands
   like lingering smoke from a lonely cigarette
   sucked up through the hum of a
   ceiling fan
   and blown out through
   its dust covered vent
   and into the streets' sidewalk runway of dreams,

   as passers by
   caught up in their daily lives
   and routine of standard tunes
   unknowingly inhale these faint
   fabled fumes
   without a clue of
   what happened on that bandstand
   just a few hours ago

on an improvisationist
full flight midnight afternoon ...

Those travellers,
many weary, from carrying
treasure cases concealing
twisted tubes of gold,
something modern
but very old,
to be blown thru
with the breath of new life
as if circling the walls Jericho
to be transformed,
reconfigured, ... and reborn
each day time night
on a bandstand near you ...
... if we let it bes
                    do ...
Those elevated,
sometimes celebrated
hallowed sound launching pads
are being replaced by HD flat screens,
thus becoming much too few,
creating a pain and anxiety that
goes beyond just payin' dues,
as griot-oral music traditions vanished
from the concrete jungles of
ghetto stoops, bar stools, and public schools ...

"And too many few"
have places,
to take the gold out of their cases,
in front of significant above ground view,
and speak a coded
        "Sankofa"
                Ancestral truth of ...

... what was ... what is ...
    ... and what will be ...
        ... if we let it bes do ...

The expansion of space and time
in between the gig
can sometimes
flip
a sage brothers wig
while in pursue to
share love,
seek acceptance ... and strive for perfection ...

The drought of appreciation,
like the lack of nourishing rain,
makes river beds dry up and crack,
as some say, "fuck dis ... an the hell with dat",
and leave,
... but not by car,
bus, bike, scooter, skateboard,
        train or plane,
they just mount that warm easy stallion
and take a slow motion ride
through a world of sub-tone sonnets of
diminished fear and pain,
in the land of nod,
holding tightly to that
magnificent breath taking horses' mane ...

And if too surreal, unreal ... slow,
then hurry up and climb the rock
... and beam them up,
to where they think they need to go;
they're in a big swig
over proof Jamaican Rum
Gypse cab rush ... can you dig,
with shirtless backs up against rented walls

trying to weather the drought of
... in between gigs ...

The creative desire of these embattled sages
has been controversial throughout the ages,
in their life long dedication
to share their improvisational intoxication ...
thus stimulating the right lobe hemispheres'
collective imagination
into "believing that anything's possible!"
while evolving toward their cosmic destinations.

Persevere, practice, meditate, and pray,
prepared and inspired
for that happnin' day,
to fire up that torch
and illuminate the collective sky, and
take your place
where so many others who've died, ... stood,
as a clear vessel for chant,
and an unshakable force for good ...

In between gigs ... can you really DIG???

the underground

alive an strugglin'
    to withstand the attitude of
    western commercial domination;

    alive an strugglin', and determined
    to musically search uncharted waters
    and explore unlabeled realms,
    while stepping out on faith
    each time to express
    uncompromisingly,
    our inner truths outer beauty –

    alive an strugglin'
    in the underground shed
    while
    practicin' an prayin'
    for the opportunity to have
    live ears instead of empty halls
    and vacant chairs for an audience;

    prayin' through practicin' for
    acceptance
    into the wide community
    of expression,
    to expose, disclose,
    reveal one's existence
    and be taken seriously –

    alive an strugglin'

    to be or not to bop,
    to crawl or not to walk,
    to look an not to see,
    to exist an not be free;

what a choice,
as the underground has no voice,
except unto themselves,

alive an strugglin'
no droppin' in a serious jugglin',
keepin' it up while holdin' it down,
job / wife /
girlfriend / kids / bills ... life,

but they shed anyway,
pondering through many-a-night,

but shed anyway,
going over the heads
then stretching out as far as they can
still linked to the bridge of tradition,

but shed anyway,
in hopes of being ever ready,
to leave a lasting impression
on those who would be blessed
enough to hear them
when they express
their collective selves;

but they shed anyway,
rethinkin',
rehearsin',
reflectin';

rethinkin',
rehearsin',
an reflectin'
on the sound,
on the spirit
of the music;
in order

to write an arrange
to re-write, an re-arrange,
after erasin' an crossin' out,
to add on an turnaround
until pleased with that statement in sound;

alive an strugglin',
they manage to faithfully meet
at least a once in a week
with their collective self,
to share
and disagree,
to agree
to play soft,
agree
to play hard,
agree
to play angry,
agree
to play love,
agree
to play joy,
an agree
to
play beautiful
for you ...

1988

facts full

FACTS full
closet of days
deep in seething brain
sinews of eloquent grandeur
silent discourse
the absolute idea

sequence to seizure

I hear the color of overtones
a blue astral node of exquisite sensation
enmeshed Ascension Instinct Sequence
and ask, what can the music
transport me to know?
Rhythmic grace
Sequence to seizure
Language to the Special Sun.

1999

tone signifies

tone signifies
fractions and particles
of fable
rehearsed before
the secret of the world
sum of the whole life
as he returns to his private music
photon-angelic
being there present
the actor
in harmonic procession

freedom

... is not chaos, or anarchy, any more than a free society implies a state of anarchy. Free improvisation is a sacred art, which relies upon the integrity of its performers to produce music that is purely of the moment in which it is created and can never be replicated.

In free improvisation it is essential to be totally focused, in the moment, as the music depends upon the awareness of its performers for its form and coherence. In a state of complete concentration on the music an extreme conscious-ness of sound is created, to the point where awareness of anything outside the music disappears. This is a wonderful, almost ecstatic state, where conscious thought is bypassed and there is a direct connection between inspiration and sounds. In this state, communication between musicians is elevated to a whole other level, and seems effortless, and pieces which are spontaneously improvised can sometimes sound highly orchestrated because of their cohesiveness, demonstrating reverse entropy to an alarming degree. In this state the layer of protective armor that we all build as we grow through life is lifted off, leaving the musician vulnerable and open and highly sensitive to all that is going on imme-diately around them and really fully existing in the present.

This is an incredible feeling, beneficial for all people, as it encourages understanding and compassion for one's fellow beings. Once the walls we have built around ourselves as individuals are broken down it is clear that the good of the individual and of society are one and the same thing, and so we must treat all beings only with sensitivity and compassion.

The laws of physics state that all matter tends toward maximum entropy: iron rusts, rocks break up, essentially, things fall apart. Life operates in direct opposition to this law, creating order from those same elements which when not animated by a soul will tend toward chaos. Life creates order, from the cellular level all the way up … this is cause for wonder, amazement.

New York, May, 2008

tel lie vis ion

Tell, Tel Lie, Tel Lie Vis, Tellivission

Refuse to go. Refuse to go.
Don't come back in a body bag. Refuse to go!

Refuse to go. Refuse to go.
Don't come back in a body bag. Refuse to go!

Is it just my imagination, is my memory bad?
Am I biased in my indignation?
Or is the news so bland, so washed like sand
We don't hear what's wrong with our own nation?
What we hear, what we see, when we watch TV
And read all the daily papyrus
Is a small lion's roar, of the need to go to war!
Before the newly created enemy attacks us!
Never mind, we can't find, can't reveal, can't admit
That there is no evidence whatever.
We'll bomb, we'll embargo, we'll blitz with propaganda.
We'll profit on each new endeavour

Now iWi is a tough guy, Texas Cowboy
He runs five miles everyday
Lets send little Georgie to run down Osama
On some lonely Afghan highway
Shouldn't be much of a match, because Georgie is intact
And Osama is sporting a catheter

But he's a marathon man well maybe Georgie can
Find him, catch him and prevent another disaster

Dick Cheney, he's somewhat of a bionic man,
Talks rough out of the side of his mouth.
Give the man a suit of Armour, send him over to the border

He'll investigate and come back with the truth!

Refuse to go. Refuse to go.
Don't come back in a body bag. Refuse to go!

Donnie Rumsfield, lean an mean,
Tough as nails, sharp as a tack
Send Rummie over there, to the desert fair,
Let him lead some other Dummies in attack.
Now Poppa George, on his 70th birthday,
Did a skydive to prove his virility.
So for 72, let him parachute thru
To Saddam's secret weapons facility.
Once he gets there, we can arrange the affair
That this conflict is really about,
A duel to the end, Bush versus Hussein.
Let the two of them sort it all out.

Don King can promote it, the Supreme Court will vote it.
We'll rebuild the Roman Colosseum (in Las Vegas).
It'll be a huge success, than the whole world can rest.
No needs for World War ad infinitum.

Refuse to go. Refuse to go.
Don't come back in a body bag. Refuse to go!

Our senators and representatives rave and rant eloquent,
To persuade their constituents to bluster.

But after so many lies, the people are more wise,
Deception must harder to muster.

Tel-Lie-Vis-Ion
The local press and the media also seem to ignore the
Dissent.
But the people still protest, and their opinions so express.
They know we are not happy and content.

Tel-Lie-Vis-Ion
The Senate and Congress, by and large
Ignored the voice of the masses. .
They received all of our calls of protest and dissent,
Then went and voted to save their own asses.
But what about the protests against another war?
It's gotten too big not to see it!
From coast to coast, from north to south,
Folks are shouting their feelings against it.
Tel-Lie-Vis-Ion

Refuse to go. Refuse to go!
Don't come back in a body bag. Refuse to go!

Not one of those Congresspersons who voted for war
Has the remotest chance of actually fighting.
They'll send in their stead (many will come back dead).
The children of our most unenlightened.
Let's send all these old men who advocate war,
To participate in the battle.
I'll bet this mess would calm down real fast,
And the old swords would cease to rattle.
Tel-Lie-Vis-Ion

Refuse to go. Refuse to go!
Don't come back in a body bag. Refuse to go!

Hey, what about these cases of corporate corruption,
And the governments complicity in them?
When's Cheney gonna give up those documents
That the courts have requested of (subpoenaed from) him?
Who cares about the recently unemployed and laid off,
And those who lost their work in nine/eleven?
While corporate outlaws are slapped on the wrist
And keep most of what they've stolen.
Greed is a bigger epidemic than aids.

The economy is swiftly declining.
But the media will focus on "W"s Hocus-Pocus,
Predicting a false silver lining.

Refuse to go. Refuse to go!
Don't come back in a body bag. Refuse to go!

Tel-Lie-Vis-Ion
The Administration can suppress any knowledge of unrest,
While the roles of poor and homeless keep on swelling.
But the media doesn't inform us
That the problems are enormous.
The psyche of war and terror is what they're selling.
Are they completely bought? Or just overwrought
By their corporate advertiser and owner?
We've trusted the Foxes to guard the Chicken farm.
Their appetites grow ever stronger.

Refuse to go, Refuse to go,
Don't come back in a body bag, refuse to go!

Tel-Lie-Vis-Ion

broken

I am a broken one.
    Sighs and tremors
    of the earth's crust
    set me shaking.
    Mere insinuations of hearts
    overflow my streams, my dreams
    fill my arroyos

    I have weather.
    I have weather.
    I am moved
    by the planetary orbs.
    I am in motion.
    I am emotion.
    I am a broken one.
    The wind shutters through me,
    plays me, like dry leaves.

    I am a broken one.

    No illusion
    of the solid here,
    I swim
    on the shifting tides.
    I move.
    I navigate.
    I am a broken one.
    I give.
    I am a broken one,
    broken open.

    broken

          open

ocean

And if I were a poet
    A poem I could make of it.
    Sitting by the ocean
    solo
    Seeing touching just a fraction of it
    And the shallows of it at that
    A message from the divine,
    "This is how deep and wide I am. Here a tiny
    peace of that magnitude that lays beyond."

    And I am shook
    to tears. Touched.

    And streaming, streaming salt tears, I walk
    into the wave churning waters,
    Where they wash back into their ocean home.

    And if I were a poet
A poem I could make of it.

poets of the now

Hoarding shards of perceptionless vibrations,
Smiling down tirelessly suffocating fears,
Crossing rivers on the backs of formless jealousies,
Climbing over the last dead, rotting insecurity.

There and then, the Now appears

Opening arms so as not to take them up,
Lifting the front end of strollers up subway stairs,
    Listening to the silence of the void,
    before the first note touches the air,
Gazing on the endless power and possibilities of the present.

    Witness this harvest of the Now
    from which such sweet fruit is bared

Glint of night retreating from newly sown seeds of breath,
From behind glass walls, fragile self-esteem steps aside
As soul reaches out, knocking it all away –
Free to connect to the world again,
Sending isolation to its lonely grave.

Yet staying vigilant, listening for the next crowding in of
thoughts,
Unwittingly ready to erect new enclosures.
What's it like to live in the past or future of your mind,
I've mostly forgot,
Confusing the Now with the fantasy of
some other place and time,
Some other experience, never resembling mine.

Maybe seeing where I am right now
is not where I'd hoped to be,
But being able to BE that NOW in THIS time

and space and KNOW
    The transitoriness of a situation
    and NOT let it determine who I am,
But to know the wholeness of it all
    And not be swept away, lost, somehow,
    in the cluttered musings of some illusion.

This is the lucidity of the immediate,
The arrival of living.

No more prisons of the mind, body or spirit,
No more how-it-is-you're-supposed-to-be police,
Rambling, ramble
Slowing, slow
Center, centering
Now, now

The five skandhas,
both simultaneously present and destroyed,
This is the challenge.

The rich, the poor,
The shuckster, the hustler,
The businessman, the homeless,
Those most proud of being gas-guzzlers.

All in need of this Now,
Not simply a bunch of words,
But something once found,
The beauty of which paves a lush path to the infinite,
Transforming the victims of the swamp into the Poets of the
    Now.

July, 2002

transitions

    Forks in the road.
Eternal moments harbor choices consciously made or
decisions instinctively followed.
Getting used to the road less traveled,
another thought, another path.
Smiling children sometimes point the way,
smooth legged women beckon with winks down other
familiar corridors.
Ears anxiously pressed to persistent, vibrating walls.
Blaring saxophones pull mind and body into new worlds,
transiting self to newly found placements of color and sound,
melting the sheaths of a now distant darkness.
Here it is, here we are.
The music creating a room of its own,
spliced onto the relative world.
As real as the ache in your heart,
replacing needs you thought you had.
All manner of sound spilling into the air,
creating palaces built of
melody and rhythm,
surrounded by swaths of dripping harmonies,
unknown to this new configuration yet deeply remembered
and comforting
in all its unfamiliarity,
altering fearfulness and restlessness into the eternal
brightness
That does not judge.
Stupid, yet wise old men say there's no avoiding it.
Acquiesce now.
Prescient trumpets blow bright yellow ribbons from
future time and space.
Open the windows, sweep away the dust, renovate.
Build new homes made of light and texture.

143

Jaki Byard said "There are many worlds."
Visit, stay, build.
Take wrecking ball to thinly parsed dogmas,
resurrect the naturalness of the being of sound.
Lakeside swans breathe sighs of relief with
     each noticed moment.

April, 2003

untitled

Last day in Demajagua
   lizards run along the walls
   after the rain, in the sun.
   One night to go on a trip to Loquillos Playa Azul.
   Perhaps! Is this the year of the dead rat?
   Anyway it's travelling but not with Delta like us.
   The ducklings have gone to Caguas with Don Luis
   and the Buddha and the privileged cock stay behind
   happy and content.

   Solange,
   the seashell and you
   are equally beautiful
   still very different
   Shadow image
   of my foot and the shape
   of Puerto Rico
   look alike
   I knew that, you said
   Sun, water and a pregnant crab
   walking at Loquillo with
   Da-deee and
   John, in the sand.

   After leaving Demajagua,
   I followed your suggestion to visit that
   strange looking star in the lower Milky Way.
   Your old, rundown space vehicle did a good job,
   it took only a week and
   a day to get there.
   On arriving, I put my ear to the rubbery surface of the
   star

and I heard a sound as if a great crowd of people came
toward me.
Then I saw an image of a naked tree shimmering in the
cold wind,
on one of its branches hung a long white feather.
This image slowly faded
and another one of black, shining buildings of
glass and steel
became my vision.
Monolith Mausoleum. Theirs or mine?

Dedicated to the Castellar Family in Brooklyn

being

how I found being
    between cause and caution
    hyphenated abbreviated double
    spaces a new sentence
    take it literally
    an end unended
    be patient with it
    sound out the syllables
    make yesterday's sense obsolete
    grammatically incorrect erased
    effaced so little effort
    exerted in an eye's blink
    a re action reinacted un invented
    only visible illusions allowed
    for this sensory perception
    because my nursery never rhymed
    only rocked inside diagrams of adverbed flesh
    agitated then arrested every syncopated season
    every cycle syntax signal
    every surface
    every skin
    every simultaneous solo starts
    with being wanted
now as much as then

Ijeoma Thomas

inside job

Broken words on concrete tongue
  no food not even water
  for this drought this famine
  This door has an eye that sees
  In not out
  Constricted cells conspiracy
  The remote we can't control
  Who wants to take the long way anymore?
  Some have forgotten
  How to walk how to run
  how to be
  hands out asking
  blood dried eyes closed
  moments melting pooling
  blurred liquefied stagnant
  sounds like an inside job
  glances glares search lights
  interrogation examination
  aiming books filled with X
  (to) move the world out of the fire
  fist curled asking
  discomforted disturbed
  memoried into memorials
  don't need a hand out
  too many without
  times up
  bruised beyond battle
  asking over weapons
  writing from the top of trees
  face turned sun
  beneath us _____
  one mind released from
the decomposing brain

148

sumotuwe
betty carter

tell it in black
 beginning to end
 an absolute wail
 silhouettes spin spiral
 gold on silver on black
 divas singing
 walls erupt without destruction
 belief explodes a wind force
 without notice the unexpected burns
 into the atmosphere balanced
 on the edge of shooting stars
 in the age of ice wearing pink
 glittered masks beauty blazing
 tell it in black
 no exchanges no refunds
 what are you gonna do
 in the extraordinary calm
 tell it before the storm
 before the grip of sudden thunder
 rattles inside the gourded throat
 sing sister until the new day comes
tell it in black

Oluyemi Thomas

being happy and aware of it

Using strength that happiness gives us is one of a kind.
The hidden powers latent therein is most interesting.
Gifts at the floor of our souls, hearts, and minds, which
makes our "strength more vital, our intellect keener and
our understanding less clouded". One could say priceless
and immeasurable are the blessings rained down upon us
if we are open to it. Even a smile sends off light, in addition
to laughter, they both release large amounts of energy that
relaxes our spirit/body.

Dig it, or get to it, before it expires.
Self-shipwreck is important, that is to find our way from the
fractured pieces that belong to us and with us. View and
review the myriad secrets deposited within.

24 April, 2008

untitled

Trusting the organic process of being human is similar to advancing down the horns or in the middle range and above the high register.

Intervals or skipping through the Iya Ilu* is such a clarifying reward. The being and doing part of living protects me from myself. Certain tests in life or learning cycles give us the opportunity to reinvest our learning into musical experience that enhances our connection with the Creator, humans, animals, vegetables, and the mineral Kingdom. Methinks, the Kingdom of Names reflects the Kingdom of the Almighty, lets continue matching / connecting them together.

28 April, 2008

* talking drum, Nigeria

Assif Tsahar

for roscoe

The sound sheets of them
    Hanging from the walls
    All different colors
    All the different signs
    For god
    We could never agree on
    Or understand
    The beauty
    As suddenly
    One note
    Played You
    All alone
There ... on stage

untitled

There is a bird
  Sitting on my tongue
  Flying is silence

        Snow melting feet
        I dream of forgetting
        Remember the dream

  There is a world
  In the palm of my hand
  Where time stood still
  An ego for an island
And tears for a sea

David S. Ware

all in before the all was

Death in livingness / Recollection / now the oblation
is so magnificent / in all the global immobile omens /
they have cursed or blessed the demons / non-virtue
stands still / the draught / the great draught of his life /
now and nothing is / is without force once in the
angel's arch / beneath star struggle and omniscient
obliqueness / for love and love a strange implantation /
sky in ruins / thinking unthinkableness /
life the blindfold path to where? /
blasphemy is bleeding / serpents rejoice /

oceanic heroes pass impossible recollections of
blessedness / space entities in dogmatic wonderment cry
his word / words / fly upon ethereal love structures /
the ground of nil is bliss / is bliss / is bliss /
seeing the perceptive aura dance and weep in unbelievable
essential amazement /

the sperm of vastness is approaching Being's womb /
now the timeless hex is the hex /
before satanic satisfaction universal kings take
thrones of cosmic copulation /

Mantels of religiousness assume positions of lordship /
horrent painful sense is in reflector stage age /
ageless knights ride original darkness
across motes of creational love sessions /
pawns of wickedness scorn wisdom hymns /
All in before the all was /

saxophone spirals

Saxophone spirals in monolithic motion
  Sleeping beauty's agnostic egg cries for mercy
   sacrificial phonetics bleed a phallic death
    Book of living Persephone
      oceanic roots gather tree of life
       submerged in smoky waters saxophone
        spirals grab for omnipotence
          swan textures contrive the transcendent
         vision upon the thighs of heaven
           Saxophone spirals echo bathe in
            intestinal foreverness
              saxology whirl thru mothers' ideational
               sandbox to where saxophone wheel
                prance across silent astral federations
                night energies frizzled horizons
                  sound ponds high step across open
                  space
                    inverted peace acres
                     herbs of inner tropical densities

spirits

Spirits prance in the universal dawn
    Spirits enhance in the astral image dawn
    Spirits dance in the causal wine
    Spirits pray in the dew of the milky way
    Spirits seek in the light of what is right
    Spirits be in the mind of HE
    Spirits nurse in the breasts of Mother Kali
    Spirits lurk in the supreme grand madness
    Spirits meet in the year of origin
Spirits awake in the day of the end of the cosmic night

who is who

There was a time when people were just people
    There was a time when nobody knew who was who
    There was no color, there was no race
    There was just people living in a space
    There was a time when the blues was all that mattered
    It was the soul of the land
    It told the story of the people
    As seen by the griots of the South
    It told a story of pain and pleasure
Passed down by words and music.

artist biographies

David Amram (17 November 1930, Philadelphia, Pennsylvania) is a composer, musician, and writer. He is a pioneer player of jazz French horn, piano, guitar, numerous flutes and is also a virtuoso on dozens of folkloric instruments as well as an inventive, improvisational lyricist. He has played with Dizzy Gillespie, Charlie Parker, Thelonious Monk, Charles Mingus, Lionel Hampton, Oscar Pettiford, Kenny Dorham, Betty Carter, Stan Getz, Nina Simone, Gerry Mulligan, Willie Nelson, Odetta, Tito Puente, Paquito D'Rivera, Arturo Sandoval, Thad Jones, Los Papines, Pete Seeger, and Machito. David has published three books and written altogether more than 100 orchestral and chamber music works, the classic scores for the films *Splendor in the Grass* and *The Manchurian Candidate*, two operas, and the score for the landmark 1959 documentary *Pull My Daisy*, narrated by novelist Jack Kerouac.

Harrison Bankhead (1 March 1955, Chicago, Illinois) is one of Chicago's most well-known bassists. He is engaged in several ensembles including 8 Bold Souls alongside Ed Wilkerson with whom he also performs in Frequency, a quartet consisting of Bankhead, flautist Nicole Mitchell, and drummer Avreal Ra. Associated through AACM they came together and released their debut album *Frequency* on Thrill Jockey Records in 2004. In the Indigo Trio (led by Mitchell) Bankhead plays with Hamid Drake, a collaboration existing since they were teenagers. Harrison has also performed with Oliver Lake, Joshua Redman, Fred Anderson, Von Freeman, The Waukegan Symphony, Roscoe Mitchell, Billy Pierce, Billy Harper, and many others.

Lewis "Flip" Barnes (21 May 1955, Norfolk, Virginia) is a trumpeter, vocalist, and integral player in any number of musical projects. He collaborates in many of William Parker's ensembles, to include: the William Parker Quartet (up front with Rob Brown and Hamid Drake), the Inside Songs of Curtis Mayfield project with Amiri Baraka, Leena Conquest, Darryl Foster, Sabir Mateen, and Dave Burrell, and the Little Huey Creative Music Orchestra. Flip's expertise also extends to dates with musicians including saxophonist Jemeel Moondoc, guitarist Jean-Paul Bourelly, vocalist and multi-instrumentalist Norah Jones, drummer William Hooker, composer Chris Becker, and ensembles like the JC Hopkins Biggish Band, Greg Tate's Burnt Sugar, The Holmes Brothers, and Noizland. Besides his work as a musician he composed and recorded the music for the films *So Many Things to Consider* and *notsoprivatethoughts*.

David Budbill (13 June 1940, Cleveland, Ohio) is a writer and musician with a lifelong passion for jazz. He was originally a student of philosophy and art history, but later graduated with a degree in theology. Several theater productions and reading tours won him acclaim as a writer. In 1999, Budbill, successful with his plays, short stories, essays, and a novel, toured nationally with William Parker performing *Zen Mountains / Zen Streets: A Duet for Poet and Improvised Bass*. David recorded *Songs For A Suffering World: A Prayer for Peace, a Protest Against War*, in 2003 with Parker and drummer Hamid Drake. His play *Judevine* has been produced dozens of times nationwide. David has received grants from the National Endowment for the Arts, the Guggenheim Memorial Foundation, and a Lifetime Achievement Award from the Vermont Arts Council. Lately, he teaches at schools and universities, and has been artist-in-residence at numerous institutions.

Katie Bull (24 December 1962, New York City, New York) is a jazz vocalist, composer, and a multimedia performance artist. While giving regular gigs at Walkers in Manhattan at the age of 15, she was introduced to jazz singer/composer Jay Clayton and singer Sheila Jordan to whom she affectionately refers as her jazz singing mentors. She is a graduate of the SUNY Purchase B.F.A. Theater Arts program. Katie has released four self-produced albums (Corn Hill Indie Label), most recently *The Story, So Far*, a CD/DVD dual release – with members of the Katie Bull Group Project Michael Jefry Stevens, Frank Kimbrough, Joe Fonda, Harvey Sorgen, Matt Wilson, Jeff Lederer, David CasT, and David Phelps – featuring an original short film with a cast of movement based improvisers. She has written and directed numerous experimental productions with her company, the Bull Family Orchestra.

Chris Chalfant (10 September 1960, Akron, Ohio) is a pianist and composer. Her influences are found in African, Hungarian, Indian, American folk, jazz, and classical music. Chris' recent project, *Book of Unstandards* (2006), is an anthology of the scores for 129 compositions she has written and a live CD, featuring her in performance with instrumentalists Joseph Jarman, Bobby Few, Connie Crothers, Pauline Oliveros, and Joseph Kubera, with vocalists Judy Bady and Thomas Buckner among others. With Jarman she founded the Lifetime Visions Orchestra and the Dojo Band. Chris produced the American Women Composers Marathon in 1989 and 1990 and the Festival of Women Improvisers, Boston, in 1991. Chalfant lives in New York City where she teaches piano, composition, and improvisation.

Jay Clayton – a.k.a. Judith Colantone – (28 October 1941, Youngstown, Ohio) is an internationally acclaimed jazz/new music vocalist, composer, and educator. Clayton has appeared alongside such artists as Muhal Richard Abrams, Steve Reich, Kirk Nurock, Julian Priester, Jerry Granelli, Jane Ira Bloom, Gary Bartz, George Cables, Fred Hersch, Gary Thomas, Urszula Dudziak, and Bobby McFerrin. She was on the jazz faculty of Cornish College of the Arts in Seattle for 20 years and is currently on the jazz faculty of Peabody Institute in Baltimore. Her accomplishments include grants from the National Endowment for the Arts, Meet the Composer, CAPS, and in 2004 she received the New Works: Creation and Performance grant from Chamber Music America. Her book, *Sing Your Story: A Practical Guide for Learning and Teaching the Art of Jazz Singing*, was published by Advance Music in 2001.

Leena Conquest (Dallas, Texas) is a singer and dancer. Her early inspirations were Ella Fitzgerald and Louis Armstrong. Leena graduated from Stanford University (Communications), attended the Tisch School of the Arts at NYU, and trained in the Alvin Ailey American Dance Theater. The virtuosity of her performances has opened opportunities for her to work across the genres: singing with Roy Ayers and Mulgrew Miller, in duet with Dave Burrell on *Leena Conquest Sings the Songs of Dave Burrell* and on his two jazz operas *Windward Passages* and *The Burrell/Larsson Songbook*, as a dancer and vocalist in William Parker's *Inside Songs of Curtis Mayfield* and *Raining on the Moon* ensemble, and on her own release *Come Fly Away.*

Cooper-Moore (31 August 1946, Piedmont, Virginia) plays piano, self-designed and constructed instruments (e.g. Diddly-Bo, Horizontal Hoe-Handle Harp, Mouth Bow, Taiser), composes, and is a storyteller. His musical aptitude as a youngster fuelled his elders' decision to nurture his passion for jazz piano. Cooper-Moore's earliest influences were Horace Silver and Ahmad Jamal. He studied composition and arranging at the Berklee College of Music in Boston, Michigan, and then moved to New York in 1973 where he began performing. He initiated different projects, like the 1992 performance *A Mindset*, his work that contrasted the American Criminal Justice and Social Welfare systems. Apogee, with David S. Ware and Marc Edwards, was his first collective improvisational trio. Currently he leads the trio Triptych Myth, with Tom Abbs and Chad Taylor. Since 2002 he has worked as a music therapist and developed the practice of teaching through music in Head Start classrooms.

Jayne Cortez (10 May 1936, Fort Huachuca, Arizona) is the author of eleven poetry books and performed her poems with music on more than nine recordings. Her engaging voice is celebrated for its political, surrealistic, dynamic innovations in lyricism and visceral sound. Jayne founded her own publishing and distribution company, Bola Press. She leads The Firespitters featuring her son Denardo Coleman and Bern Nix. Among Jayne's numerous accomplishments are two National Endowment of the Arts Fellowships, the Before Columbus Foundation American Book Award, the New York Foundation for the Arts Award, the M. Thelma McAndless Distinguished Professor in Humanities at Eastern Michigan University, and she was writer in residence and literature professor at Livingston College of Rutgers University. Cortez is organizer of the international conference *Slave Routes: The Long Memory* and director of the films *Yari Yari: Black Women Writers and the Future* and *Yari Yari Pamberi: Black Women Writers Dissecting Globalisation.* She is president of the Organization of Women Writers of Africa and is on screen in *Women In Jazz* and *Poetry In Motion.*

Connie Crothers (2 May 1941, Palo Alto, California) is an improvising pianist and composer. Her quartet features alto saxophonist Richard Tabnik, drummer Roger Mancuso, and bassists Ken Filiano or Adam Lane.

She has performed extensively as a soloist. In the trio TranceFormation, she plays with singer Andrea Wolper and Ken Filiano. Connie performed and recorded with Max Roach and Lenny Popkin. Other musical collaborators include Warne Marsh, Jemeel Moondoc, Henry Grimes, and Kevin Norton. She teaches improvisation in New York City and attended the University of Berkeley in California studying composition, then studied with Lennie Tristano. In 1972, Tristano presented Crothers in her first public performance at Carnegie Recital Hall.

Marc Edwards (23 July 1946, New York City, New York) is a NYC-based drummer and founder of the Alpha Phonics recording label. He was educated in New York City public schools. In the early '70s, Marc got to study with the great Alan Dawson at Boston's Berklee College of Music. While at Berklee he joined the group Apogee with Cooper-Moore and David S. Ware and recorded *Birth of a Being* (Hat Hut). Edwards may be best known for his work with Cecil Taylor on the landmark concert recording *Dark to Themselves* (Enja) and with David S. Ware on *Passage to Music*. His trio, with Sabir Mateen on tenor saxophone and Hilliard Greene on bass, cut the album *Red Sprites and Blue Jets* (CIMP) in 1996 and *Time & Space, Volume I* (Alpha Phonics) in 1994. Edwards formed a group with drummer Weasel Walter recording *Mysteries Beneath the Planet* (UgEXPLODE). Mark's poems and compositional notes broach the issue of spirituality and the self.

Bruce Eisenbeil (21 August 1968, Chicago, Illinois) is a composer and improvising guitarist, who started playing guitar at four and began to perform professionally when he was 15. Although primarily self-taught he studied with Joe Pass, Howard Roberts, Joe Diorio, and Dennis Sandole. Eisenbeil is distinguished by his signature sound, modern guitar techniques, and a dynamic experimental musical vocabulary with a dark harmonious nature. During his career he has had the opportunity to play with Cecil Taylor, David Murray, Milford Graves, Evan Parker, Ellery Eskelin, Andrew Cyrille, William Parker, Karl Berger, Lukas Ligeti, and many others. His trio TOTEM> includes Tom Blancarte and Andrew Drury.

Avram Fefer (9 June 1965, San Francisco, California) is a saxophonist and composer now residing in New York City. A liberal arts graduate from Harvard University, he moved to Paris in 1990, where his professional career began. He performed with Archie Shepp, Jean Jacques Avenel, Sunny Murray, John Betsch, Rasul Siddik, Kirk Lightsey, and a number of North and West African musicians, and recorded two albums. Since his move to New York City in 1995, Fefer has ten CD releases as a leader or co-leader and has performed in many ensembles – David Murray Big Band, Adam Rudolph's Organic Orchestra, Butch Morris Orchestra, Joseph Bowie Big Band, Mingus Big Band, Frank Lacy's Vibe Tribe, Michael Bisio Quartet, and Burnt Sugar. His four CD releases with master pianist Bobby Few received critical acclaim. Fefer's latest CD is *Ritual*, on Clean Feed Records (2009).

Floros Floridis (14 April 1952, Thessalonica, Greece) is a reed player and composer living in Berlin and Thessalonica. He studied physics and then clarinet at the University in Thessalonica. Floridis is the organizer of varied jazz events and a festival in Greece. He founded the label j.n.d. records, later renamed j.n.d. re-records, and has performed among others with Peter Kowald, Conny Bauer, Günter "Baby" Sommer, Evan Parker, Peter Brötzmann, Carlos Zingaro, Barry Guy, Fred Van Hove, Nicky Skopelitis, Cecil Taylor, Andrew Cyrille, Barre Phillips, and Okay Temiz. He has led 23 CDs and is been included in about 15 more. Floros composed music for the films *Annas Sommer, Faruks Café,* and *Mosconi – or to whom the world belongs* and also for theater and dance productions.

Joel Futterman (30 April 1946, Chicago, Illinois) is a pianist whose studies began by age ten. At 18 he met and studied with trumpeter Clarence Gene Shaw who introduced him to Charles Mingus. From then, he was inspired to push the limits of the piano. Joel's incessant practice regimen over the next 25 years enabled him to develop a "three hand" technique based on completely autonomous playing between the hands. Futterman has extended his instrumental repertoire to include soprano saxophone and Indian wooden flute. His discography includes over 60 recordings. He has performed throughout North America and many parts of Europe with Jimmy Lyons, Rahsaan Roland Kirk, Joseph Jarman, Hal Russell, Richard Davis, William Parker, as well as his regular working ensembles with Alvin Fielder, Edward "Kidd" Jordan, and Ike Levin.

Charles Gayle (28 February 1939, Buffalo, New York) is best known as a saxophonist, but is also an accomplished pianist, bassist, and clarinetist. His earliest performance experience was in various bars in the Buffalo area before coming to New York City. Gayle has drawn great inspiration from living and playing on the streets where he performed for several years. He has established an exceptional niche within the avant-garde scene and is celebrated internationally for his recordings with Rashied Ali and William Parker. Charles' music can be characterized as very spiritual, with numerous biblical references. Additionally, he has worked on productions with Sunny Murray, Milford Graves, and Cecil Taylor among others, and taught music at Bennington College in Bennington, Vermont. He made a name for himself internationally when, in the '90s, he toured Europe and gigged with musicians in the streets.

Alan Bernard Glover – a.k.a. Juice a.k.a. Akinjorin Omolade – (7 April 1947, Bronx, New York) is an accomplished reedman who developed his musical approach in the East Village of New York City. His loft, the Firehouse Theatre, on 11th Street and Avenue B, was a mecca of creative activity during the '70s. While learning his craft from the likes of bassist Wilbur Ware, drummer Billy Higgins, saxophonist Clarence "C" Sharpe, and other musicians, he also spotlighted and presented contemporary musicians at his music theater. His music was inspired in and by that era of political, cultural, and spiritual consciousness of the late '60s and '70s. Alan is the former leader, composer, and arranger of the Juice Quartet, a progressive contemporary jazz ensemble initially formed to record the soundtrack for an independently produced film entitled *Birth*, which he also wrote and directed.

Doug Hammond (26 December 1942, Tampa, Florida) is a drummer and composer. As a Blake High student, he played with blues and R&B bands in Tampa Bay. In Florida he performed with Earl Hooker, the 5 Royales, Little Willie John, and Sam & Dave. Invited to Detroit by Kirk Lightsey, Doug played with the Dorothy Ashby Trio, the Kirk Lightsey Trio, the Donald Byrd/Sonny Red Quintet, Chet Baker, and Focus Novii. He moved to New York and worked with James Blood Ulmer at Minton's Playhouse. Doug performed with Sonny Rollins, Charles Mingus, Ornette Coleman, Sam Rivers, Sonny Fortune, and Lonnie Liston Smith. He formed the first trio in 1977 to accompany Pony Poindexter in Europe. Hammond hired Steve Coleman and Muneer Abdul Fatah for his trio in 1981. Doug has worked mainly with his various trios, featuring Dwight Adams for the last 15 years, and recently recorded *It's Now* with Adams, Roman Filiu, and Jon Sass.

Gunter Hampel (31 August 1937, Göttingen, Germany) is a composer, bandleader, and multi-instrumentalist (vibes, bass clarinet, flute, baritone sax). As a child, Gunter studied piano, accordion, vibes, and recorder. His early exposure to jazz came after the Second World War, when Black American troops occupying Göttingen introduced him to Louis Armstrong. In 1958, Gunter started to play as a professional jazz musician. Hampel formed Birth Records in 1969 and has released 150 recordings until today. The groups he has led are the Gunter Hampel Jazz Quintet, Heartplants Quintet, and the Galaxy Dream Band. He has featured Jeanne Lee, Steve McCall, Marion Brown, Perry Robinson, Don Cherry, Cecil Taylor, Pharoah Sanders, and Anthony Braxton. Currently, he leads the Gunter Hampel European Trio and the Music & Dance Improvisation Company, that also teaches jazz improvisation workshops for children's collectives.

Jason Kao Hwang (12 May 1957, Waukegan, Illinois), a violinist, composer, and educator, has created works ranging from jazz, classical, "new", and world music. Jason's prominence on the New York scene began with Commitment, a collective quartet with saxophonist Will Connell Jr., bassist William Parker, and drummer Zen Matsuura. He went on to perform with Reggie Workman, Butch Morris, Billy Bang, Fred Hopkins, Vladimir Tarasov, Henry Threadgill, Leroy Jenkins, Makanda Ken McIntyre, Sirone, Jerome Cooper, Anthony Braxton, and many others. His chamber opera *The Floating Box: A Story In Chinatown* (New World), his recent CD *Stories Before Within* (Innova) with his jazz quartet EDGE as well as Local Lingo, his duet with kayagum musician Sang Won Park, and Spontaneous River, his improvising string orchestra, have all received critical acclaim. Jason has taught at New York University, Southern Connecticut University, Westminster College, and Brooklyn College.

Joseph Jarman (14 September 1937, Pine Bluff, Arkansas) is a multi-instrumentalist and founding member of the Association for the Advancement of Creative Musicians (AACM). Joseph played trumpet and drums in school before joining the military, where he took up saxophone. After his discharge in 1958, he met Roscoe Mitchell, and the two studied music harmony and theory at Chicago's Woodrow Wilson Junior College. There, they associated with Malachi Favors, Anthony Braxton, Henry Threadgill, Alvin Fielder, and Muhal Richard Abrams and along with Fred Anderson and Kelan Phil Cohran formed the AACM. Jarman was soon to join Don Moye, Malachi Favors, and Lester Bowie in the Roscoe Mitchell Ensemble, which became the Art Ensemble of Chicago. Joseph remained with the Art Ensemble until 1993 when he began to focus on his spirituality. After a break of three years, he joined Leroy Jenkins and Myra Melford in the trio Equal Interest and in 2003 returned to the Art Ensemble.

Terry Jenoure (22 September 1953, Bronx, New York) is a violinist, vocalist, composer, and storyteller with a keen sensitivity to theater. She leads her own ensembles, has published books and essays about improvised music and music education, teaches at Lesley University, and is director of the Augusta Savage-Gallery at the University of Massachusetts. She has presented various compositions in Europe with Leroy Jenkins at the Moers Festival (1987) and was accompanied by Herb Robertson and Kim Clarke at Berlin in 2006. Terry's music dance production with Maria Mitchell, *Josephine Baker – A Celebration of Life in Stages*, received wide critical acclaim. Terry collaborated with saxophonist Sibylle Pomorin on a tribute to beat poet Anne Waldman, recording the album *Auguries of Speed* in 1995.

Lee Konitz (13 October 1927, Chicago, Illinois) is an alto saxophonist and composer. As a child, his early influences were the big dance bands and Benny Goodman's clarinet playing. Their playing encouraged him to ask for a clarinet from which he moved to the alto saxophone, being inspired by Duke Ellington with Johnny Hodges. Konitz studied saxophone with Lennie Tristano, learned how to improvise, and developed a style noted for unorthodox phrasing. His early recordings with Stan Kenton, Miles Davis (*Birth of the Cool*), Jerry Wald, Lennie Tristano, Claude Thornhill, Gil Evans, and Gerry Mulligan were among the first of the "modern" genre. Lee's debut as a leader was with the 1949 release of *Subconscious-Lee* (Prestige). He went on to record and perform with Charles Mingus, Dave Brubeck, Ornette Coleman, Ray Nance, Elvin Jones, and many others. Konitz also contributed to the film score for *Desperate Characters* in collaboration with Ron Carter and Jim Hall.

Peter Kowald (21 April 1944, Massenberg, Germany – 21 September 2002, New York City) was an internationally acclaimed bassist. He began playing bass and tuba at 15 and by 16 had joined the Peter Brötzmann Ensemble. Soon after, he and Brötzmann toured with Carla Bley, The Globe Unity Orchestra, and made two recordings – *For Adolphe Sax* and

Machine Gun. Kowald moved on to collaborate with many improvisers – John Stevens, Evan Parker, Fred Van Hove, Han Bennink, Wadada Leo Smith, Günter "Baby" Sommer, Karl Berger, William Parker, Keith Tippett, Floros Floridis, and Joëlle Léandre. Besides playing bass with larger groups, in duets, and as a soloist, he was involved in different workshops and organizations – among them, the Sound Unity Festival in New York and his own Global Village Suite that emphasized international, cross-cultural improvisations.

Oliver Lake (14 September 1942, Marianna, Arkansas) is an alto saxophonist. He spent his childhood in St. Louis where he began artistically as a painter, then his interest in jazz led him to start playing alto saxophone. His artistic repertoire has extended to include composition, bandleading, and poetry. Oliver co-founded three of the most prestigious collectives known to modern music, the St. Louis-based Black Artists Group, The World Saxophone Quartet, and Trio 3. Lake's career as a performing musician moved to New York during the '70s and was rooted in the downtown loft scene. In 1988, Lake founded Passin' Thru Records (that is still active today) to advance knowledge, understanding, and appreciation of the arts. His compositions include those for string quartets, big band, and symphony orchestras and he has been the recipient of numerous commissions – The Guggenheim Fellowship, New Residencies Meet The Composer, Library Of Congress, and the Mellon Jazz Living Legacy.

Yusef Lateef (9 October 1920, Chattanooga, Tennessee) is a multi-instrumentalist (tenor saxophone, flute[s], oboe, bassoon, shehnai, koto), composer, and educator. His earliest recordings as a leader were in the mid-'50s for the Savoy and Prestige (New Jazz) labels. In the '60s, he toured and recorded with the ensembles of Charles Mingus, Cannonball Adderley, Miles Davis, Dizzy Gillespie, and Babatunde Olatunji. Later, he worked in collaboration with Barry Harris, Archie Shepp, Hugh Lawson, and Albert "Tootie" Heath. He studied flute, oboe, and Music Education, before becoming an Associate Professor at Manhattan Community College (New York City). By 1992, Lateef founded (and still records on) the YAL Records label, and had written a novel and short stories. His doctoral dissertation (UMass Amherst, 1975) was on Islamic and Western Education and his study prepared him to become a Senior Research Fellow at Ahmadu Bello University in Zaria, Nigeria. Lateef's works have been commissioned internationally and played by major orchestras to include the WDR Big Band, the Detroit Symphony Orchestra, and the Symphony of the New World. He is well known for teaching music from the auto-physiopsychic perspective.

Joëlle Léandre (12 September 1951, Aix-en-Provence, France) is a double bassist, improviser, and composer. Joëlle started playing double bass as a child. Through a grant from the Center for Creative and Performing Arts in Buffalo, New York, she became acquainted with the New York music scene and has worked with several improvisers and free jazz musicians, including Derek Bailey, George Lewis, William Parker, Anthony Braxton, Marilyn Crispell, Mat Maneri, Maggie Nicols, Irène Schweizer, Fred Frith, Evan Parker, Carlos Zingaro, Urs Leimgruber, Barre Phillips, Lol Coxhill, and Peter Kowald. Léandre's involvement in contemporary music was proceeded by her recordings with John Cage and Giacinto Scelsi. She was Visiting Professor and held the Darius Milhaud Chair for improvisation and composition at Mills College Oakland in 2002, 2004, and 2006. Joëlle Léandre has about 150 recordings to her credit.

Elliott Levin (23 October 1953, Philadelphia, Pennsylvania) is a saxophonist and poet. He studied music and creative writing at the University of Oregon and later studied with Cecil Taylor, saxophonist Michael Guerra, and flautist/composer Claire Polin. Over the years he has performed with Harold Melvin & The Blue Notes, The Sound of Philadelphia Band, Odean Popes' Saxophone Choir, The West Philadelphia Orchestra, New Ghost, The Warriors of the Wonderful Sound, and Talking Free Bebop. His spoken word collaborations include performances with poets Miguel Algarín, Gloria Tropp, Butch Morris' Chorus of Poets, and Frank Messina & Spoken Motion. Elliott's own poetry has been published in *L.A. Weekly*, *Blue Beat Jacket* (Japan), *The Painted Word*, *Po' Fly*, *Vital Pulse*, *Poets & Prophets*, and *Intervals: The Poems of Musicians* (Beehive & Sisyphus Press).

George E. Lewis (14 July, 1952, Chicago, Illinois) serves as the Edwin H. Case Professor of American Music at Columbia University. The recipient of a MacArthur Fellowship in 2002, an Alpert Award in the Arts in 1999, and fellowships from the National Endowment for the Arts, Lewis studied composition with Muhal Richard Abrams at the AACM School of Music, and trombone with Dean Hey. A member of the Association for the Advancement of Creative Musicians (AACM) since 1971, Lewis' work as composer and improviser includes electronic and computer music, computer-based installations, notated and improvisative forms, and is documented on more than 130 recordings. His oral history is archived in Yale University's collection of "Major Figures in American Music". His widely acclaimed book, *A Power Stronger Than Itself: The AACM and American Experimental Music* (University of Chicago Press, 2008), received many awards.

David Liebman (4 September 1946, Brooklyn, New York) plays soprano and tenor saxophones and is a composer. His career has spanned nearly four decades, beginning as a member of both the Elvin Jones and Miles Davis groups, continuing with his own bands, Lookout Farm, Quest, and the Dave Liebman Group. In jazz education he is a renowned lecturer and author of multitranslated books as well as instructional DVDs and published chamber music: *Self Portrait Of A Jazz Artist, A Chromatic Approach To Jazz Harmony And Melody*, and *Developing A Personal Saxophone Sound*. Liebman is the Founder and Artistic Director of the International Association of Schools of Jazz (IASJ), which he established in 1989 to network educators and students of jazz music through exchange programs and collaboration. He has played on nearly 300 recordings with over 100 under his leadership or co-leadership and composed several hundred original compositions.

Joseph Gabriel Esther "Joe" Maneri (9 February 1927, Brooklyn, New York – 24 August 2009, New York City, New York) was a composer, saxophonist, clarinetist, educator, and father of violinist Mat Maneri. In his youth he played with different dance bands upstate New York. Joe studied with Joseph Schmid, who was a student of Alban Berg. Joe's playing and recordings are influenced by his microtonal theories and compositions. Maneri gave courses in microtonal composition, published the workbook *Preliminary Studies in the Virtual Pitch Continuum* and taught at the New England Conservatory of Music, Massachusetts. He was invited there by Gunther Schuller, with whom he had worked in 1965. Maneri published poems, written in his own constructed language, in the anthology *Asemia* and in *Intervals*. He first used this language in 1999 on the recording *Tales of Rohnlief*. Later, Joe formed a jazz ensemble whose performances were based on Arnold Schoenberg's twelve-tone music.

Sabir Mateen (16 April 1951, Philadelphia, Pennsylvania) is a saxophonist, clarinetist, flautist, and composer who has worked on the New York City music scene since his arrival in 1989. In his youth, Sabir began playing multiple hand instruments, then as a teenager moved to flute, continually transforming his musical direction. His career perked on the '60s rhythm and blues circuit and the '70s found him in the saxophone chair of Horace Tapscott's Pan Afrikan Peoples Arkestra. Moving on to New York City, Sabir performed with Cecil Taylor, Sunny Murray, William Parker, and Alan Silva, then regularly with Daniel Carter, Butch & Wilber Morris, Raphe Malik, Steve Swell, Roy Campbell, Matthew Shipp, Jemeel Moondoc, William Hooker, and Charles Downs a.k.a. Rashid Bakr. He has been a member of several ensembles to include the quartet TEST, the Raphe Malik Quartet, One World Ensemble, and Tenor Rising/Drums Expanding. He leads The Sabir Mateen Ensemble, TRIO SABIR, and The Omni-Sound.

Nicole Mitchell (17 February 1967, Syracuse, New York) is a creative flautist, composer, and bandleader. The first woman president of the Association for the Advancement of Creative Musicians (AACM), Mitchell is a Visiting Professor at University of Illinois, Chicago. She is founder of Black Earth Ensemble and has performed throughout Europe, the U.S., and Canada. Awarded Chicagoan of the Year *(Chicago Tribune)* and Flutist of the Year (Jazz Journalist Association), Mitchell works to raise respect for flute in improvised music. She began as a classical player in her teens, and was later inspired by Jimmy Cheatham and James Newton to enter the improvisational world. Mitchell moved to Chicago in 1990, worked for Third World Press, and co-founded Samana, AACM's first all-woman band. In the late '90s, she started working extensively with Hamid Drake and David Boykin, and began leading her own projects. Mitchell has also worked with George Lewis, Anthony Braxton, Roscoe Mitchell, Fred Anderson, and Dave Douglas.

Ras Moshe (22 March 1968, Brooklyn, New York) is a tenor and alto saxophonist and has written poetry since his youth. Initial musical inspiration came from his father and grandfather, both of whom were professional musicians. He decided to make music his career in the '90s and played with Sabir Mateen, Bill Cole, William Hooker, and Steve Swell. Moshe's earliest recordings, the *Live Spirits* series, were self-produced and featured multi-reedist Joe Rigby, pianist Walden Wimberley, bassists Todd Nicholson and Matt Heyner, and drummer Jackson Krall. Moshe has curated the Music Now Festival series since 1999, where he expands his core accompanists to include Matt Lavelle, Kyoko Kitamura, and Tor Yochai Snyder. Ras recently formed the band The Ras Quartet with drummer Rashid Bakr, guitarist Dave Ross, and bassist Shayna Dulberger. They recorded the disc *Transcendence*.

Roy Nathanson (17 May 1951, Brooklyn, New York) is a saxophonist, composer, actor, poet, teacher, and bandleader of the Jazz Passengers, a group that came out of his early association with the Lounge Lizards. The Passengers have recorded eight CDs over the years and done extensive touring over their 20-year career. Roy has scored many films and theater productions for David Cole, the Public Broadcasting Service, Suzan Pitt, Jacob Burkhardt, and Tamara Jenkins. He has received two Meet the Composer grants to design collaborative programs with children. Recently, Roy has concentrated on combining text and music in a variety of ways: writing songs for performers such as Elvis Costello, Jeff Buckley, Deborah Harry, a radio play for NPR, and recording with his singing, talking, playing band Sotto Voce. His second CD with this group, *Subway Moon*, was released in 2009 as well as his first poetry book *subway moon* at buddy's knife jazzedition.

Bern Nix (21 September 1950, Toledo, Ohio) has played the guitar since the age of eleven. He taught privately in workshops in Toledo before coming to New York City. In 1975, after graduating from the Berklee College of Music in Boston, he successfully auditioned with Ornette Coleman. There, he met James Blood Ulmer and along with Ronald Shannon Jackson formed Ornette's original Prime Time band. Bern performed and recorded with Coleman from 1975 to 1987 and later became a member of Jayne Cortez' Firespitters. Nix performed with James Chance and the Contortions and appears on their 1981 *Live in New York* album. Since 1985, he has led The Bern Nix Trio whose first recording, *Alarms and Excursions* (New World Records), was released in 1993. Bern has performed with artists such as John Zorn, Marc Ribot, Elliott Sharp, Jemeel Moondoc, Kip Hanrahan and has an enduring 30 year musical relationship with Detroit saxophonist Patrick Brennan. His recent recordings, both 2006 releases, are *Low Barometer* (Tompkins Square) and *Les is More* that appears on *Art and Money* (1687, Inc).

William Parker (10 January 1952, Bronx, New York) is a bassist whose talent extends to many indigenous African string and wind instruments. William's professional preparation for his participation on the fertile New York City improvising scene came from study and early association with Richard Davis, Wilbur Ware, and Jimmy Garrison. Earliest notoriety for Parker was as bassist in the Cecil Taylor Unit. He has some 185 CDs and records on which he has performed as leader or sideman. William leads several ensembles, including Raining on the Moon, The Inside Songs of Curtis Mayfield, and The Little Huey Creative Music Orchestra. In 2007, buddy's knife jazzedition published *who owns music?*, Parker's political thoughts, poems, and musicological essays.

Matana Roberts (Chicago, Illinois) is a versatile alto saxophonist, clarinetist, and composer. She is a member of the Association for the Advancement of Creative Musicians (AACM). Inspired by early contact with established musicians, she developed the ability to project her own expressions musically. She has played in collaboration with Steve Lacy, Eugene Chadbourne, Hannah Marcus, Fred Anderson, Nicole Mitchell, Jeff Parker, Robert Barry, Joe Maneri, Miya Masaoka, Vijay Iyer, and Ralph Alessi. In 2002, she moved to New York where she played on subways and published her experiences in the 'zine *Fat Ragged*. Matana formed a trio with bassist Josh Abrams and drummer Chad Taylor and released her second recording *Sticks and Stones* in 2004. In 2008 she recorded *The Chicago Project*, that features members of Prefuse 73 and Tortoise. Roberts also composed and performs *Coin Coin*, in which she artfully sketches her family history through different media.

Larry Roland (13 July 1949, Boston, Massachusetts) is a Boston-based poet and bassist. His enthusiasm for poetry developed while he was a student at Boston University. Larry's musical journey brought him to record and perform with the Raphe Malik Quartet (that included Raphe, Sabir Mateen, and Cody Moffett). As a writer, he has published several volumes of poetry and performed spoken word at festivals to include those at Harvard University, Boston University, Massachusetts Institute of Technology, and Boston's Institute of Contemporary Art. On his first CD release as a leader, *As Time Flows On* (2008), he recites his imaginative and thought provoking poems to his own bass accompaniment.

Matthew Shipp (7 December 1960, Wilmington, Delaware) is a pianist and composer, well-known for his exhilarating style. Besides Matt's love for jazz, that he has explored since the age of twelve, he also experimented with contemporary classical music, hip hop, and electronica. At the New England Conservatory of Music he studied with Joe Maneri and had lessons with Dennis Sandole. He came to New York in 1984 where he joined the downtown avant-garde scene, playing with the David S. Ware Quartet and the Roscoe Mitchell's Note Factory. In the '90s, he released several chamber jazz albums on the Swiss Hatology Label. He performed with William Parker's Other Dimensions in Music and formed the Matthew Shipp String Trio (with Mat Maneri and William Parker). Matt directs the Blue Series and has also recorded a collection of multifaceted works for Thirsty Ear records.

Catherine Sikora (Cork, Ireland) is a tenor saxophonist whose playing is deeply influenced by poetry and her indigenous music. Since working her way to New York to study abstract improvisation, coming from a completely music-free schooling in Ireland, she performs regularly around the metropolitan area, both as a leader and as a sideman. Current projects include Clockwork Mercury with Eric Mingus, a duo project with Jeremy Bacon, 22 with Matt Lavelle, and the Catherine Sikora Trio with François Grillot and Bob Hubbard.

Warren Smith (13 May 1934, Chicago, Illinois) is a drummer and multi-instrumentalist. He recorded with Miles Davis in 1957, and concurrently taught at the Third Street Settlement, Adelphi University, and SUNY College at Old Westbury. A few years earlier, Smith studied music at Manhattan School of Music. In the late '70s, Warren opened his loft, Studio Wis, where NYC-based improvising musicians such as Wadada Leo Smith and Oliver Lake recorded. He was a founding member of two stellar organizations: the Composers Workshop Ensemble and M'Boom with Max Roach, and performed with Sam Rivers, Gil Evans, Anthony Braxton, Charles Mingus, Henry Threadgill, Joe Zawinul, Tony Williams Lifetime, and the Untempered Ensemble of Bill Cole. Warren's expertise brought him work outside the jazz genre, accompanying Aretha Franklin, Nina Simone, Lloyd Price, Nat King Cole, Van Morrison, and Janis Joplin. In 1998, he released his solo album *Cats Are Stealing My Shit* and in 2004 *Race Cards*, where he jams with saxophonist Andrew Lamb, Mark Taylor on French horn, and Tom Abbs on bass.

Lisa Sokolov (1954, Roslyn, New York) is a jazz vocalist, improviser, and composer. She began as a classical pianist and vocalist, but soon became absorbed in the music of John Coltrane. Lisa located bassist Jimmy Garisson at Bennington College, Vermont, and once there, she studied with Bill Dixon, Jimmy Lyons, Milford Graves, Vivian Fine, and Louis Calabro. She joined the New York music scene in 1977 collaborating with bassist William Parker, working in trio with Ellen Christie and Jeanne Lee. Sokolov has been heard with Cecil Taylor, Rashied Ali, Badal Roy, Andrew Cyrille, Wayne Horvitz, Jimmy Lyons, Irène Schweizer, Gerry Hemingway, Butch Morris, Didi Jackson, Cameron Brown, and Hilton Ruiz. She is a full professor at New York University, Tisch School of the Arts, Experimental Theatre Wing. Her method of Embodied VoiceWork is of great significance in arts education, music therapy, and human potential work. She has recorded as a leader on Laughing Horse Records and also, as featured vocalist, on *Song Cycle* of William Parker (Boxholder) and *Songs* of Gerry Hemingway (Between the Lines).

Steve Swell (6 December 1954, Newark, New Jersey) is a trombonist and composer. He plays in the ensembles Slammin' the Infinite, Fire Into Music, Unified Theory Of Sound, and the Nation of We (NOW) Ensemble. Soon after Steve arrived in New York in 1975, he found work in the bands of Buddy Rich and Lionel Hampton, joined Makanda Ken McIntyre's band,

and performed in Bob Fosse's Broadway production Dancin'. He recorded with Tim Berne, Joey Baron, Alan Silva, Herb Robertson, Jemeel Moondoc, Anthony Braxton, Cecil Taylor, William Parker, Bill Dixon, Butch Morris, John Zorn, Elliott Sharp, Rob Mazurek, and Perry Robinson. He studied with Roswell Rudd, who is one of his influences, with Grachan Moncur III, and with Jimmy Knepper. Steve teaches in New York City public schools.

John Tchicai (28 April 1936, Copenhagen, Denmark) is one of Europe's first free jazz saxophonists. He studied at the Academy of Music in Aarhus, Denmark. In the early '60s he came to New York where he co-founded the New York Contemporary Five, the New York Art Quartet, and The Jazz Composers Guild. After returning to Denmark a few years later, he played with Cadentia Nova Danica, but then concentrated on working as a teacher of music education. In 1975, a performance of John and pianist Irène Schweizer was recorded and released as *Willi The Pig*. He led different ensembles, such as John Tchicai and the Archetypes, in San Francisco, where he moved to in the early '90s. In his career Tchicai has worked with John Coltrane, Don Cherry, Archie Shepp, John Lennon/Yoko Ono, Johnny Dyani, Roswell Rudd, Albert Ayler, Abdullah Ibrahim – a.k.a. Dollar Brand –, Makaya Ntshoko, Carla and Paul Bley, Misha Mengelberg, Lee Konitz, and Cecil Taylor. Tchicai is a member of Wadada Leo Smith's Yo Miles and lives today in France, where he experiments with electronics in his music.

Ijeoma Thomas (17 August 1950, Washington D.C.) is a vocalist, poet, and performance artist. She is co-leader of the band Positive Knowledge performing and recording with her husband Oluyemi. Ijeoma has toured nationally (East and West Coasts) and internationally in Africa, Asia, and Europe. She is a graduate of Hampton University. Thomas has performed as a vocalist with Cecil Taylor, Roscoe Mitchell, William Parker, Alan Silva, Kidd Jordan, and Sunny Murray. Her poetry is collected in the book *Out of the Fire* and is featured in numerous publications. Ijeoma is the founder and director of Poetry out Loud, a literacy project for children and youth.

Oluyemi Thomas (16 August 1952, Detroit, Michigan) is a multireedist and leader of the ensemble Positive Knowledge, a band in which he performs alongside his wife Ijeoma, the vocalist and poet. With her he has also worked in trio with bassist Henry Grimes. Oluyemi studied at Washtenaw College in Ann Arbor, Michigan, where he received his degree in Mechanical Engineering and worked as a mechanical engineer. He also studied music, and was especially interested in African Music. Besides Positive Knowledge, Thomas works with his African Drum units as a soloist, and in various trio/duo settings with musicians to include Cecil Taylor, Wadada Leo Smith, Alan Silva, William Parker, Sunny Murray, Kidd Jordan, Wilber Morris, Michael Wimberly, John Tchicai, Roscoe Mitchell, Anthony Braxton, and Charles Gayle.

Assif Tsahar (11 June 1969, Tel Aviv, Israel) is a saxophonist and clarinetist. Assif grew up in Tel Aviv where he began playing the guitar as a teenager before switching to saxophone. At 21, he traveled to New York where he stayed and began to play with different musicians on the improvised music scene. In 1999, he founded Hopscotch Records, which is a non-profit organization where recording artists have unparalleled freedom over their productions. On Hopscotch he released productions of the Assif Tsahar Brass Reeds Ensemble, the KJLA String Quartet, and different works of musicians including Rashied Ali, Peter Kowald, Cooper-Moore, Hamid Drake, and Tatsuya Nakatani. He has produced numerous performances of improvisers on the New York music scene and released many of their recordings.

David S. Ware (7 November 1949, Plainfield, New Jersey) is a saxophonist well-known for his own ensemble – the David S. Ware Quartet with Matthew Shipp, William Parker, and Guillermo E. Brown. The Quartet released 20 albums receiving critical acclaim and performed at festivals and venues throughout Europe and North America. David practiced with Sonny Rollins in earlier years. He attended the Music School in Boston and played there with Stanton Davis, Cedric Lawson, Art Lande, and Michael Brecker. In Boston Ware also met Cooper-Moore and Marc Edwards with whom he formed the trio Apogee. He later became a member of the Cecil Taylor Unit, Andrew Cyrille's Maono, and Beaver Harris' 360° Ensemble. When Sonny Rollins was inducted into the Nesuhi Ertegun Jazz Hall of Fame in 2005, the David S. Ware Quartet was asked by Rollins to perform part of his *Freedom Suite* (AUM Fidelity) that had been recorded a few years earlier. In 2009, David recorded *Shakti* (AUM Fidelity) with Joe Morris, William Parker, and Warren Smith.

Henry P. Warner (15 July 1940, New York City, New York) is a saxophonist and clarinetist. As a child Henry began with playing the trombone and later added saxophone and clarinet. His arrival on the New York Loft scene in the '70s is marked by the band he formed: The Bakery. Henry's close musical associations with William Parker and Billy Bang culminated in his earliest recording sessions and he has also played or recorded with Frank Lowe, Jemeel Moondoc, Sun Ra, Zane Massey, Roy Campbell, Earl Freeman, Elder Abishai Ben Reuben, Wayne Horwitz, Art Jenkins, Rashid Bakr, Sunny Murray, Charles Tyler, Wilbur Ware, Clarence "C" Sharpe, Denis Charles, Evelyn Blakey, Ellen Christie, Lisa Sokolov, Kali Z. Fasteau, Andrew Lamb, Blaise Siwula, Sadiq Abdu Shahid, Lewis Barnes, Gene Cooper, Snoop Dogg, John Jones, Ibrahim Gonzalez, Sam Gresham, Reggie Workman, Warren Smith, and others. His two recordings as a leader are *Blue Nile IV: The Art of the Ensemble* (2002) and *Vibrational Therapists – The Radius of the Mind* (2003).

references for previously published pieces
quellenangaben zuvor veröffentlichter texte

Amram, David; the woman in the black beret
Previously published in: *Nine Lives of a Musical Cat*, Paradigm Publishers, 2007

Chalfant, Chris; swan song
Previously published in: *Book of Unstandards*, 2004

Cortez, Jayne; keys to the city and mambo lesson
Previously published in: *Jazz Fan Looks Back*, Hanging Loose Press, 2003

Kowald, Peter; untitled
Previously published in: *Was da ist*, CD, 1994
Translation: Isabel Seeberg & Paul Lytton

Roland, Larry; the underground
Previously published in: *As Time Flows On*, CD, 2001

Smith, Warren; tel lie vis ion
Previously published in: *Race Cards*, CD, 2003